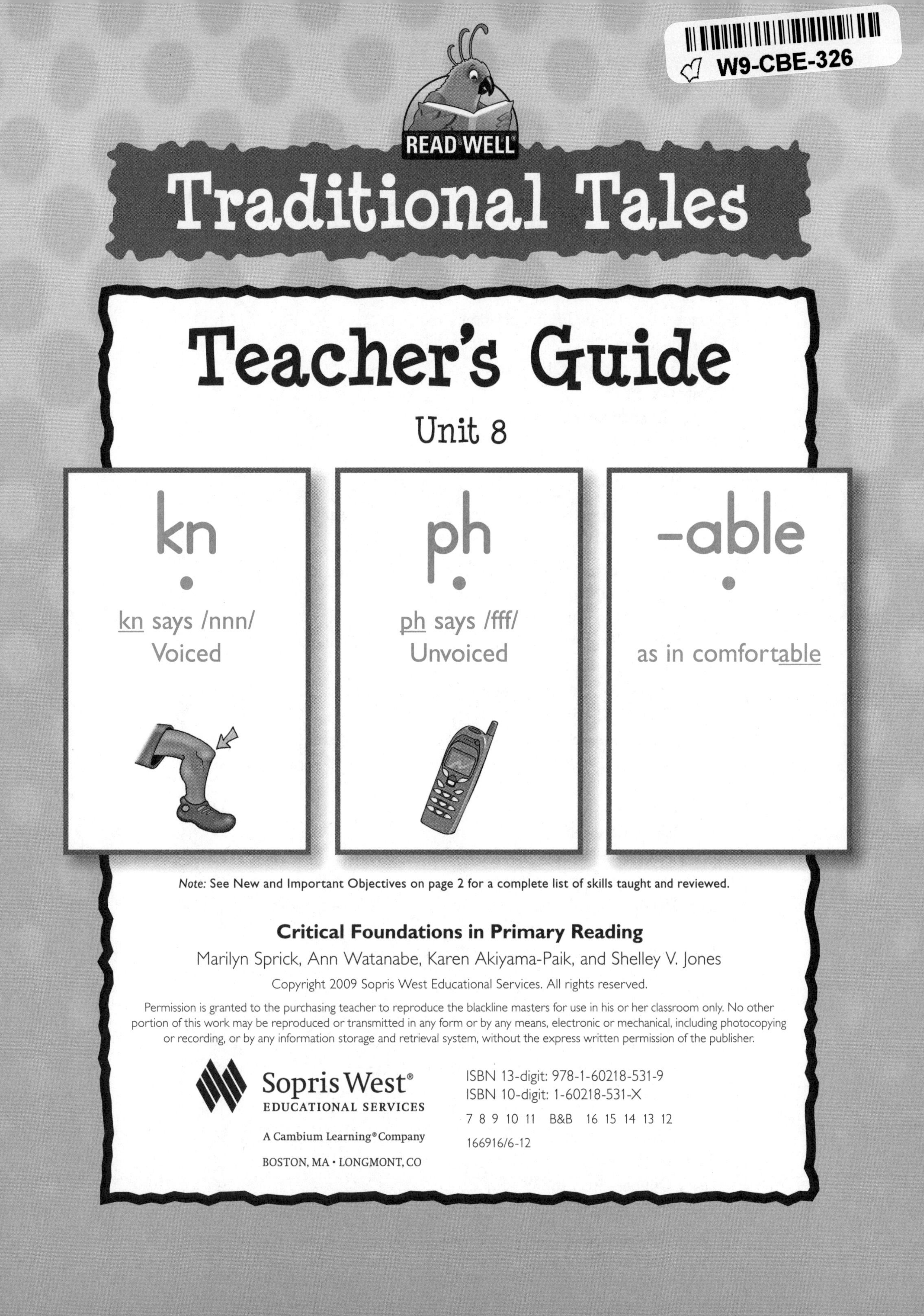

Traditional Tales

Teacher's Guide

Unit 8

Note: See New and Important Objectives on page 2 for a complete list of skills taught and reviewed.

Critical Foundations in Primary Reading

Marilyn Sprick, Ann Watanabe, Karen Akiyama-Paik, and Shelley V. Jones

Sopris West® EDUCATIONAL SERVICES
A Cambium Learning® Company
BOSTON, MA • LONGMONT, CO

ISBN 13-digit: 978-1-60218-531-9
ISBN 10-digit: 1-60218-531-X
7 8 9 10 11 B&B 16 15 14 13 12
166916/6-12

Table of Contents
Unit 8
Traditional Tales

How to Teach the Lessons

End of the Unit

Letter Sounds and Combinations

Cumulative Review of *Read Well 1* Sounds and Combinations (Ss, Ee, ee, Mm, Aa, Dd, th, Nn, Tt, Ww, Ii, Th, Hh, Cc, Rr, ea, sh, Sh, Kk, -ck, oo, ar, wh, Wh, ĕ, -y as in fly, Ll, Oo, Bb, all, Gg, Ff, Uu, er, oo as in book, Yy, a schwa, Pp, ay, Vv, Qq, Jj, Xx, or, Zz, a_e, -y as in baby, i_e, ou, ow as in cow, ch, Ch, ai, igh, o_e, ir) and:

Unit	Letters	Sound	Key Word	Type
Unit 2	aw	/aw/	**Paw**	Voiced
Unit 3	ew	/o͞o/	**Crew**	Voiced
Unit 3	ue	/o͞o/	**Blue**	Voiced
Unit 3	u_e	/o͞o/	**Flute**	Bossy E Voiced
Unit 5	ow	/ōōō/	**Snow**	Voiced (Long)
Unit 6	ge	/j/	**Page**	Voiced
Unit 6	-dge	/j/	**Badge**	Voiced
Unit 7	ci	/sss/	**Circle**	Unvoiced
Unit 7	ce	/sss/	**Center**	Unvoiced
Unit 8	kn	/nnn/	**Knee**	Voiced
Unit 8	ph	/fff/	**Phone**	Unvoiced
Unit 10	oa	/ōōō/	**Boat**	Voiced (Long)
Unit 11	oi	/oi/	**Point**	Voiced
Unit 11	ea	/ĕĕĕ/	**Bread**	Voiced (Short)
Unit 12	gi	/j/	**Giraffe**	Voiced
Unit 12	au	/au/	**Astronaut**	Voiced
Unit 13	oy	/oy/	**Boy**	Voiced

Affixes (including morphographs—affixes taught with meaning) and Open Syllables

Cumulative Review of *Read Well 1* Affixes (-ed, -en, -es, -ing, -ly, -s, -y, -tion) and:

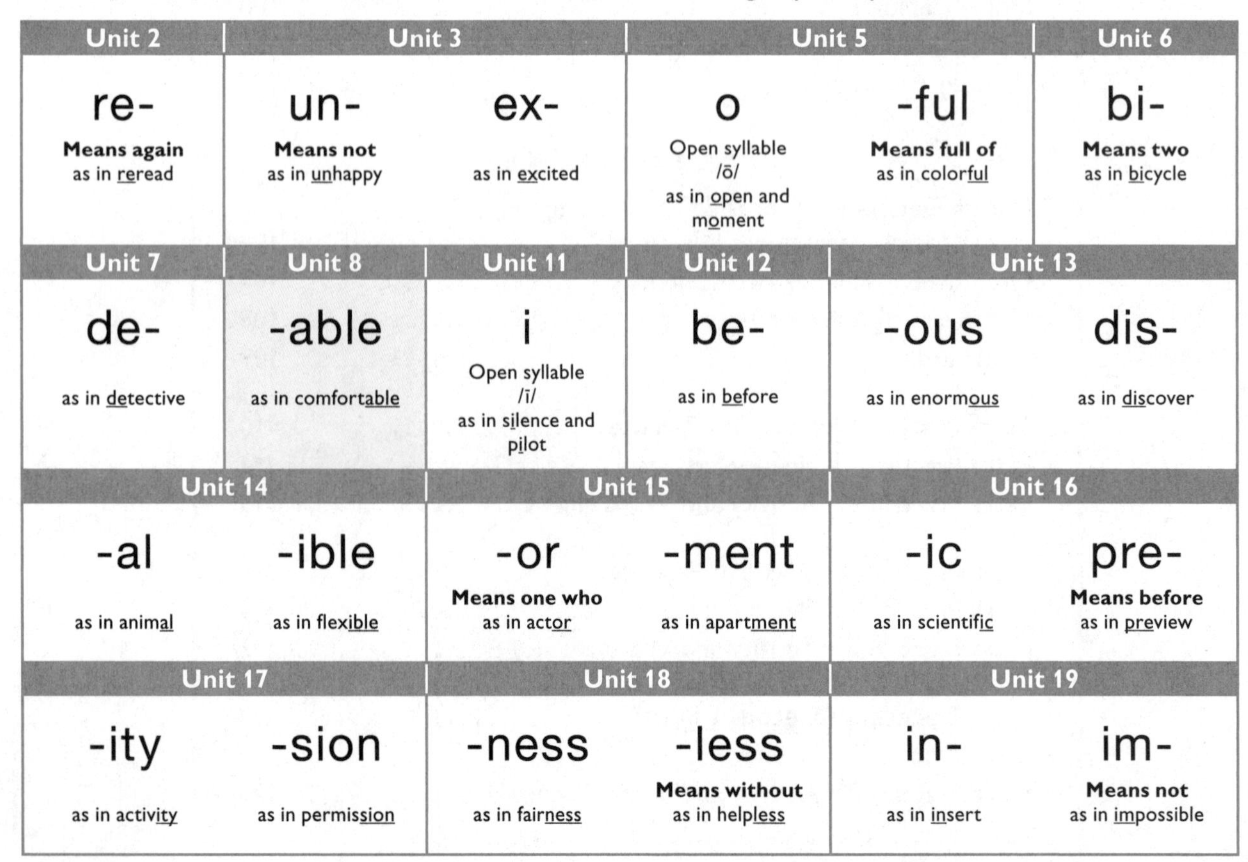

Unit	Affix	Meaning	Example
Unit 2	re-	**Means again**	as in reread
Unit 3	un-	**Means not**	as in unhappy
Unit 3	ex-		as in excited
Unit 5	o	Open syllable /ō/	as in open and moment
Unit 5	-ful	**Means full of**	as in colorful
Unit 6	bi-	**Means two**	as in bicycle
Unit 7	de-		as in detective
Unit 8	-able		as in comfortable
Unit 11	i	Open syllable /ī/	as in silence and pilot
Unit 12	be-		as in before
Unit 13	-ous		as in enormous
Unit 13	dis-		as in discover
Unit 14	-al		as in animal
Unit 14	-ible		as in flexible
Unit 15	-or	**Means one who**	as in actor
Unit 15	-ment		as in apartment
Unit 16	-ic		as in scientific
Unit 16	pre-	**Means before**	as in preview
Unit 17	-ity		as in activity
Unit 17	-sion		as in permission
Unit 18	-ness		as in fairness
Unit 18	-less	**Means without**	as in helpless
Unit 19	in-		as in insert
Unit 19	im-	**Means not**	as in impossible

Introduction
Traditional Tales

Story Notes

Through Miss Tam's journeys, students have learned that people all over the world share the tradition of storytelling. In this unit, students read two stories that follow the oral folktale tradition. Both stories transcend time and place as they teach important lessons about people.

The Emperor and the Seed: In this classic tale, students learn about the importance of integrity through the Emperor's quest to find a successor. A young peasant boy is rewarded for doing his best and telling the truth. The supportive and gentle relationship between the boy and his grandfather emphasizes *Read Well*'s theme of family.

Stone Soup: Lessons on sharing, community, and trust are taught through this traditional tale about minstrels, a village, and a pot of soup. Students will enjoy reading the story as a three-act play, complete with narrator, chorus, minstrels, and villagers.

Recommended Read Alouds

The *Read Well 2* suggested Read Alouds enhance small group instruction—providing opportunities to further build background knowledge and vocabulary.

CAUTION
(Reminder)
Do not read the Read Aloud recommendations during small group instruction. Reserve this time for students to read.

The Empty Pot by Demi
Fiction • Folktale
The Empty Pot is another retelling of the traditional tale "The Emperor and the Seed."

Cactus Soup by Eric A. Kimmel
Fiction • Folktale
Cactus Soup is a Mexican variant of the "Stone Soup" story, complete with a glossary that defines Spanish words used in the book.

***Read Well* Connections**
The Read Alouds demonstrate how traditional tales evolve through retelling yet retain their timeless lessons. Students can compare these versions with the ones they read, noting similarities and differences.

NOTE FROM THE AUTHORS

GENRE

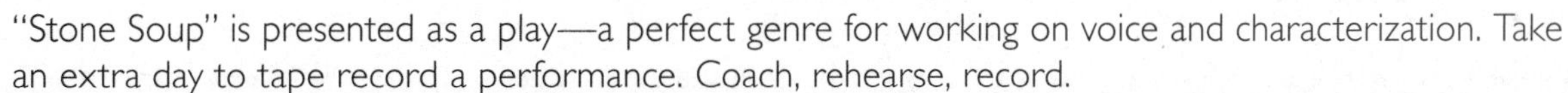
"Stone Soup" is presented as a play—a perfect genre for working on voice and characterization. Take an extra day to tape record a performance. Coach, rehearse, record.

New and Important Objectives

A Research-Based Reading Program

Phonemic Awareness
Phonics
Fluency
Vocabulary
Comprehension

Phonological and Phonemic Awareness

Segmenting; Blending; Rhyming; Onset and Rime;
Counting Syllables

Phonics

Cumulative Letter Sounds and Combinations

Review • Ss, Ee, ee, Mm, Aa, Dd, th, Nn, Tt, Ww, Ii, Th, Hh, Cc, Rr, ea, sh, Sh, Kk, -ck, oo, ar, wh, Wh, ĕ, -y (as in fly), Ll, Oo, Bb, all, Gg, Ff, Uu, er, oo (as in book), Yy, a (schwa), Pp, ay, Vv, Qq, Jj, Xx, or, Zz, a_e, -y (as in baby), i_e, ou, ow (as in cow), ch, Ch, ai, igh, o_e, ir, aw, ew, ue, u_e, ow (as in snow), ge, -dge, ci, ce

Cumulative Affixes, Morphographs, and Open Syllables

Review • -ed, -en, -er, -es, -est, -ing, -ly, -s, -y, -tion, re-, un-, ex-, o, -ful, bi-, de-

★New Letter Sounds, Combinations, Affixes, and Morphographs

kn (as in knee) • knee, kneel, knees, knife, knock, knot, knotted, knowing, known, knows
ph (as in photo) • alphabet, graph, Phillip, Phillip's, photo, photograph
-able (as in comfortable) • comfortable, dependable, drinkable, likable, noticeable, readable

★New Proper Nouns

Cedric, China, Emperor, Jess, Jun, Jun's, Meg

★New Pattern Words

bench, brag, bragged, broth, chose, chosen, hush, inch, inched, lute, match, mush, patch, peace, plum, plums, poke, pot, pots, race, salt, salted, sense, sensed, snip, spare, spoon, spoons, square, stale, stare, strum, strummed

* **Known Pattern Words With Affixes**, **Known Tricky Words With Affixes**, and **Known Multisyllabic Words With Affixes** have base words students have previously read. The words are new in this unit because they have not been previously read with the affix.

★= New in this unit

Phonics *(continued)*

*__Known Pattern Words With Affixes__ • bakes, brings, chopped, chops, closer, cracked, cuts, darker, doors, finest, formed, freshly, gazed, grows, hugged, meals, placed, planted, plants, pruned, pruning, raise, raised, ruled, setting, sharing, silks, smells, staring, steaming, stones, stretched, taken, tasted, weeded

★New Compound and Hyphenated Words

grandson, grandson's, hand-painted, homemade, outsiders, sunlight

★Other New Multisyllabic Words

advice, blossoms, celery, comfort, content, crackle, crackled, departed, despite, determined, doctor, empire, empty, enter, entered, fairness, flutter, fluttered, gathering, graceful, hungry, hurried, hurry, instruments, integrity, invite, invited, medicine, minstrel, minstrels, muffins, notice, palace, practice, rapid, rapidly, recorder, remained, salad, simple, successor, summon, summoned, surprise

*__Known Multisyllabic Words With Affixes__ • excitement, happiness, kindness, returned, togetherness, traveler, villagers, villages, whispering, whispers, windows

★New Tricky Words

able, ah, appreciate, boiling, bread, carrot, carrots, certain, character, characters, curious, disappointed, embarrassed, enough, fancy, joy, lie, luscious, merry, music, narrator, patient, potatoes, poured, quiet, rewarded, scarce, scrumptious, shall, shoulders, soup, spread, taught, tied, toes, warmed, wealthy, wear, young

*__Known Tricky Words With Affixes__ • beloved, boy's, discovered, given, greatest, honesty, swarmed, watching, watered

Fluency

Accuracy, Expression, Phrasing, Rate

Vocabulary

New • advice, ancient, appreciate, brag, curious, despite, disappointed, embarrassed, emperor, folktale, imagine, integrity, luscious, merry, minstrel, scarce, scrumptious, successor, summon, village, wealthy, wonderful

Review • contented, generation

Reviewed in Context • bittersweet, commotion, community, contented, neighborhood, ordinary, plain, plead, respect

Comprehension

Unit Genres

Fiction • Folktale

Comprehension Processes

Build Knowledge: Factual, Procedural, Conceptual

Day	1	2	3	4	5	6	7
Remember							
Defining				S			
Identifying (recalling)	E,S,C	S,C	S,C	S,C	S	S,C	C
Using	S	S		S			
Understand							
Defining (in your own words)	E,S	S		C	C	S	
Describing	S	C	C	S	S	S	
Explaining (rephrasing)	S	S,C	S,C	S,C	S	S,C	
Illustrating	E,C		C		C	C	
Sequencing		C	C			C	
Summarizing		C	S,C				
Using	E,S,C	S,C		S,C	C	S	C
Visualizing	E,C		C		C	S,C	
Apply							
Demonstrating							
Explaining (unstated)	S	S		S		S	C
Illustrating	E						
Inferring	E,S	S		S	S	S	C
Making Connections (relating)	S			S	S	S	
Predicting	S	S		S	S	S	
Using	S	S,C		S,C	S	S	
Analyze							
Classifying	S						
Comparing/Contrasting			S			S	
Distinguishing Cause/Effect							
Drawing Conclusions	S	C	S			S	
Inferring		C					
Evaluate							
Making Judgments					S		
Responding (personal)	C		S,C	S		C	
Create							
Generating Ideas					S		

E = Exercise, S = Storybook, C = Comprehension & Skill

Comprehension *(continued)*

Skills and Strategies

Day	1	2	3	4	5	6	7
Priming Background Knowledge							
Setting a Purpose for Reading	S			S			
Answering Questions	S	S	S	S	S	S	
Asking Questions				S			
Visualizing							
Comprehension Monitoring/Fix Ups							
Does it Make Sense?		C		E	C	C	
Looking Back							
Restating							
Summarizing							
Main Idea							
Retelling			C			S	
Supporting Details							
Understanding Text Structure							
Title, Author, Illustrator	S	S		S		S	
Fact or Fiction							
Genre (Classifying)	S			S			
Narrative							
Setting	E,S,C	C	C	S,C			
Main Character/Traits (Characterization)*	S,C	S,C	C	S,C	S		C
Goal	S,C	C	S,C	S,C	S	S	
Problem/Solution		S,C	S,C				
Action/Events/Sequence	C	C	S,C	C	S	S	C
Outcome/Conclusion		C	S,C			S	
Lesson/Author's Message		S	S	S		S	
Expository							
Subject/Topic						C	
Heading							
Supporting Details (Facts/Information)						C	
Main Idea						C	
Using Graphic Organizers							
Chart							
Diagram (labeling)				C			
Hierarchy (topic/detail)						C	
K-W-L							
Map (locating, labeling)							
Matrix (compare/contrast)			S			C	
Sequence (linear, cycle, cause and effect)							
Story Map		C					
Web	C	C					

E = Exercise, S = Storybook, C = Comprehension & Skill

* Narrator

Comprehension *(continued)*

Study Skills

Day	1	2	3	4	5	6	7
Alphabetical Order					C		
Following Directions						C	
Locating Information							
Note Taking							
Previewing							
Reviewing		S			S	S	
Test Taking				C			C
Using Glossary		S			S		
Using Table of Contents	S						
Viewing	S			S			
Verifying							

Writing in Response to Reading

Day	1	2	3	4	5	6	7
Sentence Completion	C		C	C	C	C	C
Making Lists						C	
Sentence Writing			C			C	C
Story Retell/Summary			C			S	
Fact Summary							
Paragraph Writing							
Report Writing							
Open-Ended Response	C						
Creative Writing							

Writing Traits

(Addressed within the context of Writing in Response to Reading)

Day	1	2	3	4	5	6	7
Ideas and Content							
Elaborating/Generating			C,S				
Organization							
Introduction							
Topic Sentence							
Supporting Details							
Sequencing		C	C				
Word Choice							
Sophisticated Words (Tier 2 and 3)							
Conventions							
Capital	C		C	C		C	C
Ending Punctuation	C		C	C	C	C	C
Other (commas, quotation marks)							
Presentation							
Handwriting		C	C		C	C	
Neatness		C	C		C	C	

E = Exercise, S = Storybook, C = Comprehension & Skill

Daily Lesson Planning

LESSON PLAN FORMAT

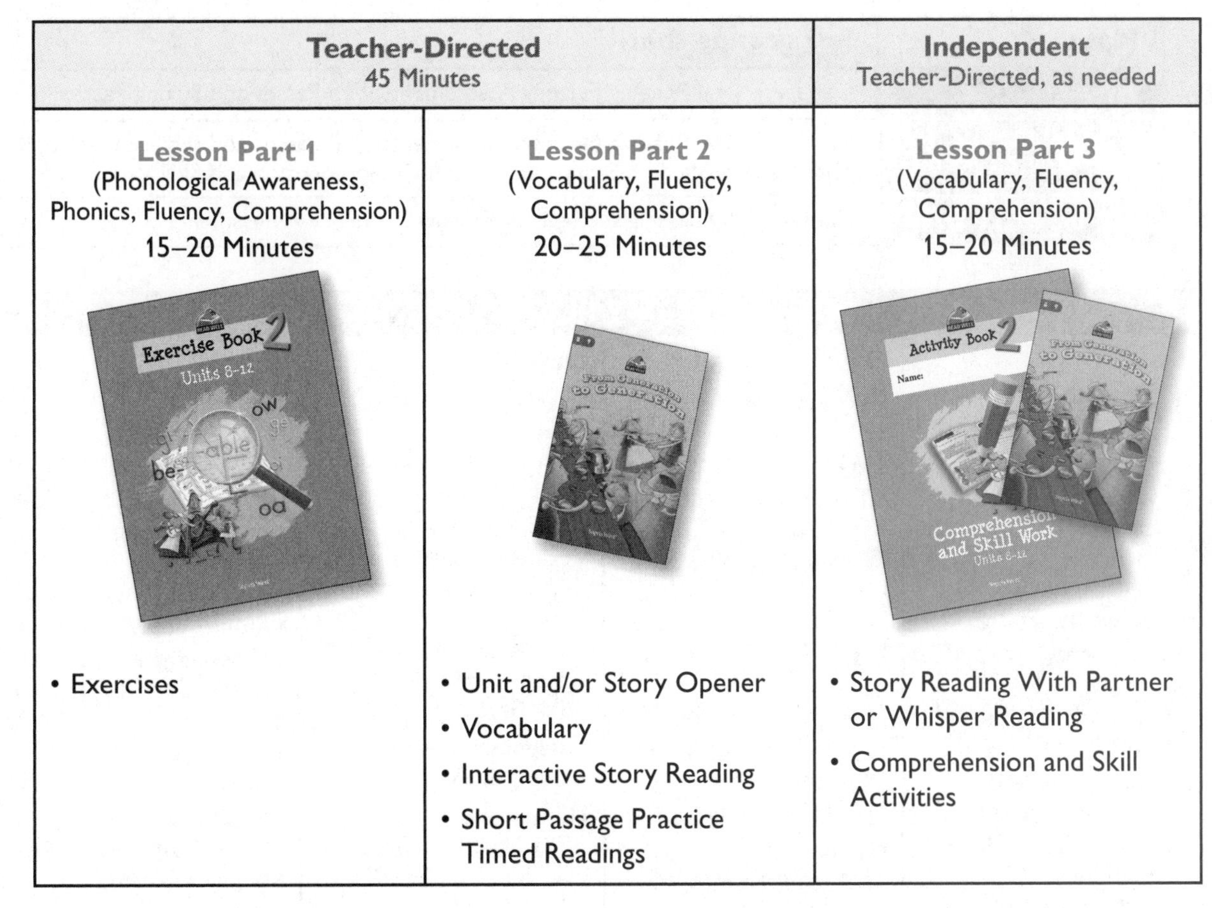

Teacher-Directed 45 Minutes		**Independent** Teacher-Directed, as needed
Lesson Part 1 (Phonological Awareness, Phonics, Fluency, Comprehension) 15–20 Minutes	**Lesson Part 2** (Vocabulary, Fluency, Comprehension) 20–25 Minutes	**Lesson Part 3** (Vocabulary, Fluency, Comprehension) 15–20 Minutes
• Exercises	• Unit and/or Story Opener • Vocabulary • Interactive Story Reading • Short Passage Practice Timed Readings	• Story Reading With Partner or Whisper Reading • Comprehension and Skill Activities

HOMEWORK

Read Well Homework (blackline masters of new *Read Well 2* passages) provides an opportunity for children to celebrate accomplishments with parents. Homework should be sent home on routine days.

ORAL READING FLUENCY ASSESSMENT

Upon completion of this unit, assess each student and proceed to Unit 9, as appropriate.

WRITTEN ASSESSMENT

During the time students would normally complete Comprehension and Skill Activities, students will be administered a written assessment that can be found on page 59 in the student's *Activity Book 2*.

Note: See Making Decisions for additional assessment information.

DIFFERENTIATED LESSON PLANS

The differentiated lesson plans illustrate how to use materials for students with various learning needs. As you set up your unit plan, always include *Read Well 2* Exercises and Story Reading on a daily basis. Unit 8 includes 7-, 8-, 9-, 10-, and 11-Day Plans.

Plans	For groups that:
7-DAY	Complete Oral Reading Fluency Assessments with Passes and Strong Passes
8-DAY	Complete Oral Reading Fluency Assessments with Passes and require teacher-guided assistance with Story Reading and Comprehension and Skill Work
9-, 10-, or 11-DAY	Have difficulty passing the unit Oral Reading Fluency Assessments

7-DAY PLAN			
Day 1 **Teacher-Directed** • Exercise 1a • Exercise 1b: Focus Lesson • Unit and Story Opener: Traditional Tales, The Emperor and the Seed • Vocabulary, Ch. 1, 2 • The Emperor and the Seed, Ch. 1 • Guide practice, as needed, on Comp & Skill 1, 2 **Independent Work** • On Your Own: Partner or Whisper Read, The Emperor and the Seed, Ch. 2 • Comp & Skill 1, 2 **Homework** • Homework Passage 1	**Day 2** **Teacher-Directed** • Exercise 2 • Vocabulary, Ch. 3 • The Emperor and the Seed, Ch. 3 • Guide practice, as needed, on Comp & Skill 3, 4 **Independent Work** • Repeated Reading: Partner or Whisper Read, The Emperor and the Seed, Ch. 3 • Comp & Skill 3, 4 **Homework** • Homework Passage 2	**Day 3** **Teacher-Directed** • Exercise 3 • Reread The Emperor and the Seed, Chapters 1–3 • Focus Lesson: Character Comparison Matrix • Guide practice, as needed, on Comp & Skill 5a, 5b **Independent Work** • Comp & Skill 5a, 5b **Homework** • Teacher's Choice	**Day 4** **Teacher-Directed** • Exercise 4a • Exercise 4b: Focus Lesson • Story Opener: Stone Soup • Vocabulary, Acts 1, 2 • Stone Soup, Act 1 • Guide practice, as needed, on Comp & Skill 6, 7 **Independent Work** • Repeated Reading: Partner or Whisper Read, Stone Soup, Act 1 • Comp & Skill 6, 7 **Homework** • Homework Passage 3
Day 5 **Teacher-Directed** • Exercise 5 • Stone Soup, Act 2 • Guide practice, as needed, on Comp & Skill 8, 9 **Independent Work** • Repeated Reading: Partner or Whisper Read, Stone Soup, Act 2 • Comp & Skill 8, 9 **Homework** • Homework Passage 4	**Day 6** **Teacher-Directed** • Exercise 6 • Vocabulary, Act 3 • Stone Soup, Act 3 • Focus Lesson: Story Comparison • Guide practice, as needed, on Comp & Skill 10, 11 **Independent Work** • Repeated Reading: Partner or Whisper Read, Stone Soup, Act 3 • Comp & Skill 10, 11 **Homework** • Homework Passage 5	**Day 7** **Teacher-Directed** • Exercise 7 • Repeated Reading: Stone Soup, Acts 1–3 **Independent Work** • Repeated Reading: Selected act from Stone Soup • Written Assessment • Oral Reading Fluency Assessment* **Homework** • Comp & Skill Activity 8 (Fluency Passage)	

* The Oral Reading Fluency Assessments are individually administered by the teacher while students are working on their Written Assessments.

8-DAY PLAN			
Day 1 **Teacher-Directed** • Exercise 1a • Unit and Story Opener: Traditional Tales, The Emperor and the Seed • Vocabulary, Ch. 1, 2 • The Emperor and the Seed, Ch. 1 • Guide practice, as needed, on Comp & Skill Activity 1 **Independent Work** • Repeated Reading: Partner or Whisper Read, The Emperor and the Seed, Ch. 1 • Comp & Skill Activity 1 **Homework** • Teacher's Choice	**Day 2** **Teacher-Directed** • Review Exercise 1a • Exercise 1b: Focus Lesson • The Emperor and the Seed, Ch. 2 • Guide practice, as needed, on Comp & Skill 2 **Independent Work** • Repeated Reading: Partner or Whisper Read, The Emperor and the Seed, Ch. 2 • Comp & Skill 2 **Homework** • Homework Passage 1	**Day 3** **Teacher-Directed** • Exercise 2 • Vocabulary, Ch. 3 • The Emperor and the Seed, Ch. 3 • Guide practice, as needed, on Comp & Skill 3, 4 **Independent Work** • Repeated Reading: Partner or Whisper Read, The Emperor and the Seed, Ch. 3 • Comp & Skill 3, 4 **Homework** • Homework Passage 2	**Day 4** **Teacher-Directed** • Exercise 3 • Review selected Vocabulary, Ch. 1–3 • Reread The Emperor and the Seed, Ch. 1–3 • Focus Lesson: Character Comparison Matrix • Guide practice, as needed, on Comp & Skill 5a, 5b **Independent Work** • Comp & Skill 5a, 5b **Homework** • Teacher's Choice
Day 5 **Teacher-Directed** • Exercise 4a • Exercise 4b: Focus Lesson • Story Opener: Stone Soup • Vocabulary, Acts 1, 2 • Stone Soup, Act 1 • Guide practice, as needed, on Comp & Skill 6, 7 **Independent Work** • Repeated Reading: Partner or Whisper Read, Stone Soup, Act 1 • Comp & Skill 6, 7 **Homework** • Homework Passage 3	**Day 6** **Teacher-Directed** • Exercise 5 • Stone Soup, Act 2 • Guide practice, as needed, on Comp & Skill 8, 9 **Independent Work** • Repeated Reading: Partner or Whisper Read, Stone Soup, Act 2 • Comp & Skill 8, 9 **Homework** • Homework Passage 4	**Day 7** **Teacher-Directed** • Exercise 6 • Vocabulary, Act 3 • Stone Soup, Act 3 • Focus Lesson: Story Comparison • Guide practice, as needed, on Comp & Skill 10, 11 **Independent Work** • Repeated Reading: Partner or Whisper Read, Stone Soup, Act 3 • Comp & Skill 10, 11 **Homework** • Homework Passage 5	**Day 8** **Teacher-Directed** • Exercise 7 • Repeated Reading: Stone Soup, Acts 1–3 **Independent Work** • Repeated Reading: Stone Soup, Acts 1–3 • Written Assessment • Oral Reading Fluency Assessment* **Homework** • Comp & Skill Activity 8 (Fluency Passage)

9-, 10-, or 11-DAY PLAN • *Intervention* For Days 1–8, follow 8-Day plan. Add Days 9, 10, 11 as follows:		
Day 9 Extra Practice 1 **Teacher-Directed** • Decoding Practice • Fluency Passage **Independent Work** • Activity and Word Fluency A **Homework** • Fluency Passage	**Day 10 Extra Practice 2** **Teacher-Directed** • Decoding Practice • Fluency Passage **Independent Work** • Activity and Word Fluency B **Homework** • Fluency Passage	**Day 11 Extra Practice 3** **Teacher-Directed** • Decoding Practice • Fluency Passage **Independent Work** • Activity and Word Fluency A or B • Oral Reading Fluency Assessment* **Homework** • Fluency Passage

Materials and Materials Preparation

Core Lessons

Teacher Materials

READ WELL 2 MATERIALS

- Unit 8 Teacher's Guide
- Sound Cards
- Unit 8 Oral Reading Fluency Assessment found on page 107
- Group Assessment Record found in the *Assessment Manual*

SCHOOL SUPPLIES

Stopwatch or watch with a second hand

Student Materials

READ WELL 2 MATERIALS (for each student)

- *From Generation to Generation* storybook
- *Exercise Book 2*
- *Activity Book 2* or copies of Unit 8 Comp and Skill Work
- Unit 8 Written Assessment found in *Activity Book 2*, page 59, and on the blackline master CD
- Unit 8 Certificate of Achievement (BLM, page 108)
- Unit 8 Goal Setting (BLM, page 109)
- Unit 8 Homework (blackline masters)
  See *Getting Started* for suggested homework routines.

SCHOOL SUPPLIES

Pencils, colors (optional—markers, crayons, or colored pencils)

Make one copy per student of each blackline master, as appropriate for the group.

Note: For new or difficult Comprehension and Skill Activities, make overhead transparencies from the blackline masters. Use the transparencies to demonstrate and guide practice.

FOCUS LESSONS

For Exercises 1b and 4b (Focus Lessons), make overhead transparencies from the blackline masters, write on transparencies placed over the pages, or use paper copies to demonstrate how to complete the lessons.

Extra Practice Lessons

CAUTION

Use these lessons only if needed. Students who need Extra Practice may benefit from one, two, or three lessons.

Student Materials

READ WELL 2 MATERIALS (for each student, as needed)

See Extra Practice blackline masters located on the CD.

- Unit 8 Extra Practice 1: Decoding Practice, Fluency Passage, Word Fluency A, and Activity
- Unit 8 Extra Practice 2: Decoding Practice, Fluency Passage, Word Fluency B, and Activity
- Unit 8 Extra Practice 3: Decoding Practice, Fluency Passage, Word Fluency A or B, and Activity

SCHOOL SUPPLIES

Pencils, colors (markers, crayons, or colored pencils), highlighters

Important Tips

Think and Talk

Unit 8 introduces Think and Talk, end-of-chapter questions that engage students in discussions about the story. Think and Talk questions review central story elements and important facts, prompt discussions that require inferential thinking, encourage students to ask questions, and ask for personal responses.

BASIC PROCEDURES

Think and Talk Example

Say something like:

Everyone, read question 1.
(Who is the main character?)
What's the answer? (the Emperor)
Yes, the Emperor is the main character.

> Gray-text questions and the sequence of Think and Talk questions prepare students for inferences.

Item 2 says "Describe the Emperor."
How would you describe the Emperor?
(He was good. He was the ruler.
He needed a successor.)
Those are all great descriptions.
I get the feeling that the Emperor was a good man who was well liked. Thumbs up if you think you would like the Emperor.

> Think aloud with students. Guide comprehension monitoring.

I wonder why I have that feeling.

It seems like the book told us some other things about the Emperor.
Let's look back in the book and see if there are words that tell us that the Emperor was well liked.

> Guide rereading to deepen comprehension.

Turn to page 10. Everyone, read the first sentence.
(In ancient times, there was a wise and beloved Emperor.)
Ah, the book told me the Emperor was beloved.
That must mean he was loved by the people.
There's another word in the sentence that tells about the Emperor. What is it? (wise)
Yes, the Emperor was wise, so he must have made good decisions.
Read one more sentence. (He ruled the land with fairness and kindness.)
Ah, what does it mean to be fair? (You don't cheat. You are nice . . .)

> Prime background knowledge.

WITH THE TEACHER

The Emperor walked in the quiet of his garden. He thought to himself, "The boys wear the finest silks. They are from the best of families. They all show me the greatest respect, but they all seem the same. What shall I do?"

The Emperor could hear the hum of the bees. The graceful plum blossoms fluttered in the gentle wind. They almost seemed to whisper. Finally, in the peace of his garden, the Emperor knew what he would do.

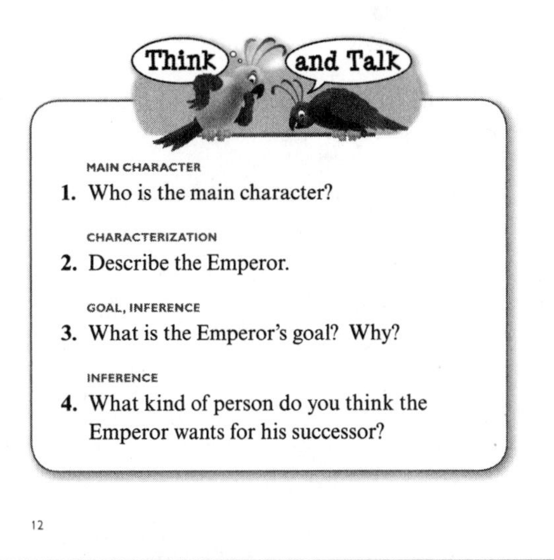

MAIN CHARACTER
1. Who is the main character?

CHARACTERIZATION
2. Describe the Emperor.

GOAL, INFERENCE
3. What is the Emperor's goal? Why?

INFERENCE
4. What kind of person do you think the Emperor wants for his successor?

12

Storybook, Unit 8
The Emperor and the Seed

All students benefit when everyone is actively engaged. Partner Think and Talk will get *all* your students to think and talk about what they read.

PARTNER THINK AND TALK PROCEDURES

1. Assign students partners.
2. Assign each partner a number, Partner 1 or Partner 2. (If you have an uneven number of students, one set of students will have two Partner 2s.)
3. Have students choral read a question.
   We're going to Think and Talk with our partners about what we just read.
   Touch question 1. Everyone, read the question and think about the answer.
4. Assign one partner to start.
   Now, discuss the answer with your partner.
   Partner 1, it's your turn first.
5. After an appropriate amount of time, based on the complexity of the response, have the other partner share.
   Partner 2, now it's your turn to . . . [restate the question].
6. Call on a student to respond.
   [Stacia], how did you and your partner answer the question?

Partner Think and Talk: Monitor comprehension, use fix-up strategies, and keep your students engaged!

Think and Talk Example (*continued*)

Everyone, read question 4 and think about the answer.
(What kind of person do you think the Emperor wants for his successor?)

Partner 1, turn to Partner 2. Tell your partner what kind of person you think the Emperor wants for his successor.

Wait for students to think and talk. Partner 2, turn to Partner 1. Tell your partner what kind of person you think the Emperor wants for his successor.

Wait for students to think and talk. [Angelina], what did you and your partner decide?
(We think the Emperor wants his successor to be fair.)
[Juan], what did you and your partner decide?
(We think the Emperor would want his successor to be kind.)
[Josh], what else did you and your partner come up with?
(We think he would want his successor to be wise.)

Very nice—if the new emperor is all of those things, I think that he will be loved by the people too. I wonder if the Emperor will be able to find such a successor.

Excellent partner work. You put your heads together and came up with very wise answers.

Sufficient amounts of instructional time support comprehension-building discussions. Think and Talk engages students in those discussions.

How to Teach the Lessons

Teach from this section. Each instructional component is outlined in an easy-to-teach format.

Exercise 1a

- Exercise 1b: Focus Lesson
- Unit and Story Opener: Traditional Tales, The Emperor and the Seed
- Vocabulary
- Story Reading 1
  With the Teacher: Chapter 1
  On Your Own: Chapter 2
- Comprehension and Skill Activities 1, 2

Exercise 2

- Vocabulary
- Story Reading 2
  With the Teacher: Chapter 3
- Comprehension and Skill Activities 3, 4

Exercise 3

- Story Reading 3
  With the Teacher: Reread Chapters 1–3
- Character Comparison Matrix: Focus Lesson
- Comprehension and Skill Activity 5a, 5b

Exercise 4a

- Exercise 4b: Focus Lesson
- Story Opener: Stone Soup
- Vocabulary
- Story Reading 4
  With the Teacher: Act 1
- Comprehension and Skill Activities 6, 7

Exercise 5

- Story Reading 5
  With the Teacher: Act 2
- Comprehension and Skill Activities 8, 9

Exercise 6

- Vocabulary
- Story Reading 6
  With the Teacher: Act 3
- Oral Story Comparison: Focus Lesson
- Comprehension and Skill Activities 10, 11

Exercise 7

- Story Reading 7
  With the Teacher: Reread Acts 1–3
- Written Assessment

PACING

Exercise 1a should take about 10 minutes, allowing about 10 minutes for the Visualizing and Illustrating Focus Lesson.

1 SOUND REVIEW

Use selected Sound Cards from Units 1–7.

★2 NEW SOUND INTRODUCTION

- For Row A, say something like:

  Look at the picture. Say "k-n says /nnn/ as in knee." (k-n says /nnn/ as in knee)
  Read the sentence. (I know a song called *Head, Shoulders, Knees, and Toes.*)
  What two words have the /nnn/ sound? (know, knees)

- For Row B, have students read the underlined sound, then the word.
- After reading the row, have students go back and read the whole words.

3 ACCURACY AND FLUENCY BUILDING

E1. Tricky Words

- For each Tricky Word, have students use known sounds and word parts to silently sound out the word. Use the word in a sentence to help with pronunciation.
- If the word is unfamiliar, tell students the word. Then have students say, spell, and say it.

ancient

The first word is *ancient*. Say the word. (ancient) Spell *ancient*. (a-n-c-i-e-n-t)
Ancient means very, very old. The queen's palace was very, very old. It was . . . ancient.
Say the word three times. (ancient, ancient, ancient)

beloved

Look at the next word. You already know a small word in this word.
What small word do you know? (love) Sound out the word in your head.
Someone who is loved is . . . *beloved*. Yes, the word is *beloved*.

shall	I don't know what to do. What . . . *shall* . . . I do?
certain	I know I had my book on the bus. I am . . . *certain*.
wear	I looked in my closet and wondered, "What shall I . . . *wear?*"
young	The boy was only five years old. He was very . . . *young*.
tied	I wrapped the string around the package and then . . . *tied* . . . it in a bow.
brought	I gathered my belongings and . . . *brought* . . . them with me.
thought	We were able to solve the problem after we . . . *thought* . . . about it.

- Have students go back and read the whole words in the column.

4 MULTISYLLABIC WORDS

For each word, have students read the word by parts, then read the whole word. Use the word in a sentence, as appropriate.

successor	Joe took over Jane's job. He was her . . . *successor*.
emperor	The Chinese ruler was called the . . . *emperor*.
summoned	We were called to court. We were . . . *summoned*.
blossoms	The magnolia tree had beautiful white . . . *blossoms*.
remained	Almost everyone left. Only two people . . . *remained*.
returned	Jason came back. He . . . *returned*.

★ = New in this unit

★5 GENERALIZATION: READING NEW WORDS IN PARAGRAPHS

- Have students read the paragraph silently, then out loud. Tell students to use the sounds and word parts they know to read any difficult words.
- Repeat practice, as needed.

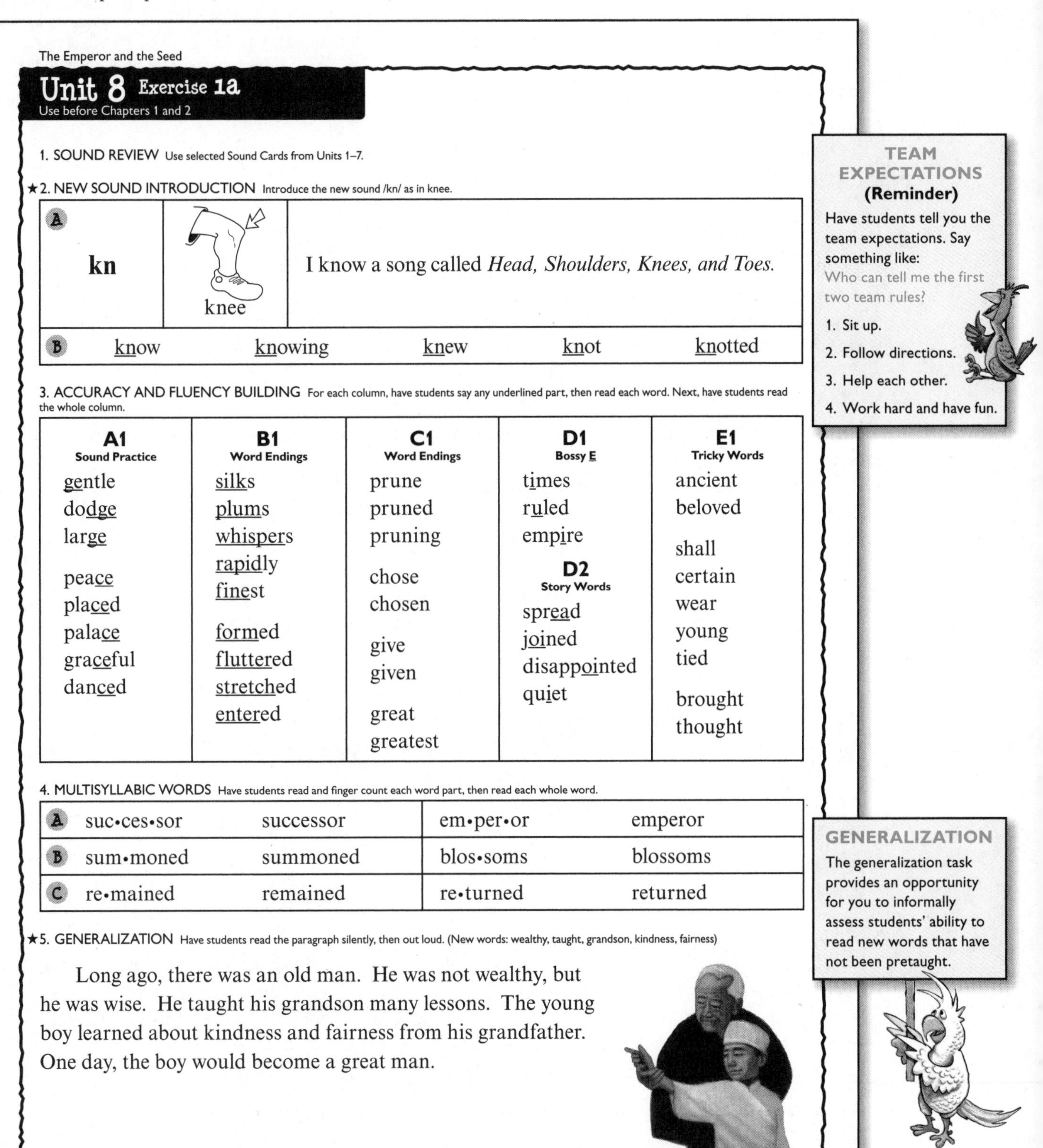

The Emperor and the Seed

Unit 8 Exercise 1a
Use before Chapters 1 and 2

1. SOUND REVIEW Use selected Sound Cards from Units 1–7.

★2. NEW SOUND INTRODUCTION Introduce the new sound /kn/ as in knee.

A **kn**	knee	I know a song called *Head, Shoulders, Knees, and Toes.*

B	know	knowing	knew	knot	knotted

3. ACCURACY AND FLUENCY BUILDING For each column, have students say any underlined part, then read each word. Next, have students read the whole column.

A1 Sound Practice	B1 Word Endings	C1 Word Endings	D1 Bossy E	E1 Tricky Words
gentle	silks	prune	times	ancient
dodge	plums	pruned	ruled	beloved
large	whispers	pruning	empire	
	rapidly		**D2 Story Words**	shall
peace	finest	chose	spread	certain
placed		chosen	joined	wear
palace	formed		disappointed	young
graceful	fluttered	give	quiet	tied
danced	stretched	given		
	entered			brought
		great		thought
		greatest		

4. MULTISYLLABIC WORDS Have students read and finger count each word part, then read each whole word.

A	suc•ces•sor	successor	em•per•or	emperor
B	sum•moned	summoned	blos•soms	blossoms
C	re•mained	remained	re•turned	returned

★5. GENERALIZATION Have students read the paragraph silently, then out loud. (New words: wealthy, taught, grandson, kindness, fairness)

Long ago, there was an old man. He was not wealthy, but he was wise. He taught his grandson many lessons. The young boy learned about kindness and fairness from his grandfather. One day, the boy would become a great man.

1

TEAM EXPECTATIONS (Reminder)

Have students tell you the team expectations. Say something like:
Who can tell me the first two team rules?

1. Sit up.
2. Follow directions.
3. Help each other.
4. Work hard and have fun.

GENERALIZATION

The generalization task provides an opportunity for you to informally assess students' ability to read new words that have not been pretaught.

★VISUALIZING AND ILLUSTRATING

FOCUS LESSON
Skills and Strategies

PREP NOTE

To demonstrate how to complete the matching exercise, use an overhead of page 2 in students' *Exercise Book 2*, write on a transparency placed over the page, or use a paper copy.

PURPOSE

This lesson provides explicit instruction in the skill of visualization. The lesson prepares students for Comprehension and Skill Work. Students do not write in their books but will watch and respond as you guide them through the lesson.

COMPREHENSION PROCESSES

Remember, Understand, Apply

PROCEDURES

1 INTRODUCTION

Explain the purpose of the lesson and what visualizing and illustrating are. Say something like:

Today, we're going to learn how to visualize and then illustrate our story. *Visualize* is a big word that means "to make a picture in your mind." Making pictures in your mind will help you understand what you read. Once you have a picture in your mind, you can draw that picture.

2 VISUALIZING AND ILLUSTRATING

Identifying—Who, Setting; Inferring; Defining and Using Vocabulary—splendid, ancient, emperor, ordinary

- Have students read the sentence in the box.

  Read the sentence. (In ancient China, a wise and beloved emperor lived in a splendid palace.)
  Who is the sentence about? (an emperor)
  The sentence also tells us about the setting.
  What country did the Emperor live in? (China) When did he live in China? (long, long ago)
  That's right. We know he lived long, long ago because the sentence says "in *ancient* China."
  Did the Emperor live in a house? (no) Where did he live? (in a splendid palace)

- Guide students through visualizing what the setting looks like. Say something like:

  Let's think about how we might illustrate that sentence. Close your eyes.
  Try to imagine the palace in your book. Was it an ordinary building? (no)
  What made it splendid? (It was large. It had a slanted roof. It looked like it belonged to someone wealthy.)
  Yes, you are right. The palace wasn't ordinary. It was outstanding. It was . . . *splendid.*

  I see beautiful trees around the palace.
  What do you see? (beautiful flowers in the garden, a wall around the palace . . .)

- Guide students through visualizing what the Emperor looks like.
- Demonstrate how you would illustrate the sentence with a simple but detailed line drawing.

  Keep your picture in your mind. It will help you make a great drawing of the sentence.
  Help me draw my picture. I think I'll start with the Emperor. Then I'll draw the palace behind him.
  First I'll start with his head. **Draw the Emperor's head.** Next I think I'll draw his robe . . .
  How can I add details to the Emperor? (give him a hat, add a mustache and beard . . .)

  Draw a picture of the Emperor, adding details that your students suggest. Then draw a palace.

  Visualizing helps you think about and understand what you've read.

★= New in this unit

You will visualize and draw what you read about today. As we read, pay careful attention to how the artist visualized and drew the Emperor and his palace.

COMPREHENSION PROCESSES

Remember, Understand, Apply

PROCEDURES

1. Introducing the Unit and Story

Identifying—Title, Main Character; Using Vocabulary—generation, folktale; Using Table of Contents; Inferring—Setting; Viewing; Classifying—Genre

Tell students the title of their new unit and story.
Say something like:
Today we start a new storybook. Look at the cover.
What is the title of our new storybook?
(From Generation to Generation)
In each family, there are grandparents, parents, and children.
The grandparents are a generation. The parents are a generation, and the children are a . . . *generation.*
What do we call each age group? (a generation)
That's right. This storybook is going to be about things that are passed from one generation to the next.

Everyone, turn to page 2. What's on this page? (the Table of Contents)
Touch the unit title.
What's the title of this unit?
(Traditional Tales)

Can you find the first story in the unit?
What is it called?
(The Emperor and the Seed)
Who is this story about?
(the Emperor)
That's right. Look at the picture.
Where do you think the Emperor might be from? (Japan, China . . .)
What makes you think the Emperor may be from Japan or China?

This story is a very old Chinese folktale.
A *folktale* is a story that people tell each other and pass along from one generation to the next.

Like many folktales, "The Emperor and the Seed" teaches an important lesson.

Do you think this story is nonfiction or fiction?
What makes you think it's [fiction]?

TABLE OF CONTENTS
UNIT 8 • **Traditional Tales**

2

2. Introducing the Title Page

Have students look at the picture on page 7. Ask questions as indicated by the gray text.

Everyone, turn to page 7, the title page of our new story . . .

3. Introducing the Author

Identifying—Author, Illustrator

Discuss the author and illustrator. Say something like:

It says the story is retold by Marilyn Sprick. That means she wrote the story down, but people have been telling it since ancient times. Who is the illustrator? (Robert McGuire)

4. Setting a Purpose

To encourage students' interest in the story's lesson, say something like:

This story is one of my favorite stories. At the end of the story, I will be excited if you can tell me two things. First, I'll be interested to see if you can explain the snazzy word *integrity*. Everyone, say the word. (integrity) *Integrity* is a very important word.

Then I'll be interested to see if you can explain the lesson that the Emperor teaches his people and why it is important.

❶ **Apply:** Inferring—Setting (The story takes place long ago in China . . .)

❷ **Apply:** Predicting; **Understand:** Explaining (We will learn an important lesson. We will learn the lesson that the Emperor teaches his people.)

COMPREHENSION PROCESSES

Remember, Understand

PROCEDURES

Introducing Vocabulary

★ancient ★emperor
★successor ★wealthy
★disappointed ★summon

- For each vocabulary word, have students read the word by parts, then read the whole word.
- Read the student-friendly explanations to students as they follow with their fingers. Then have students use the vocabulary word by following the gray text.
- Review and discuss the photos and illustrations.

USING VOCABULARY

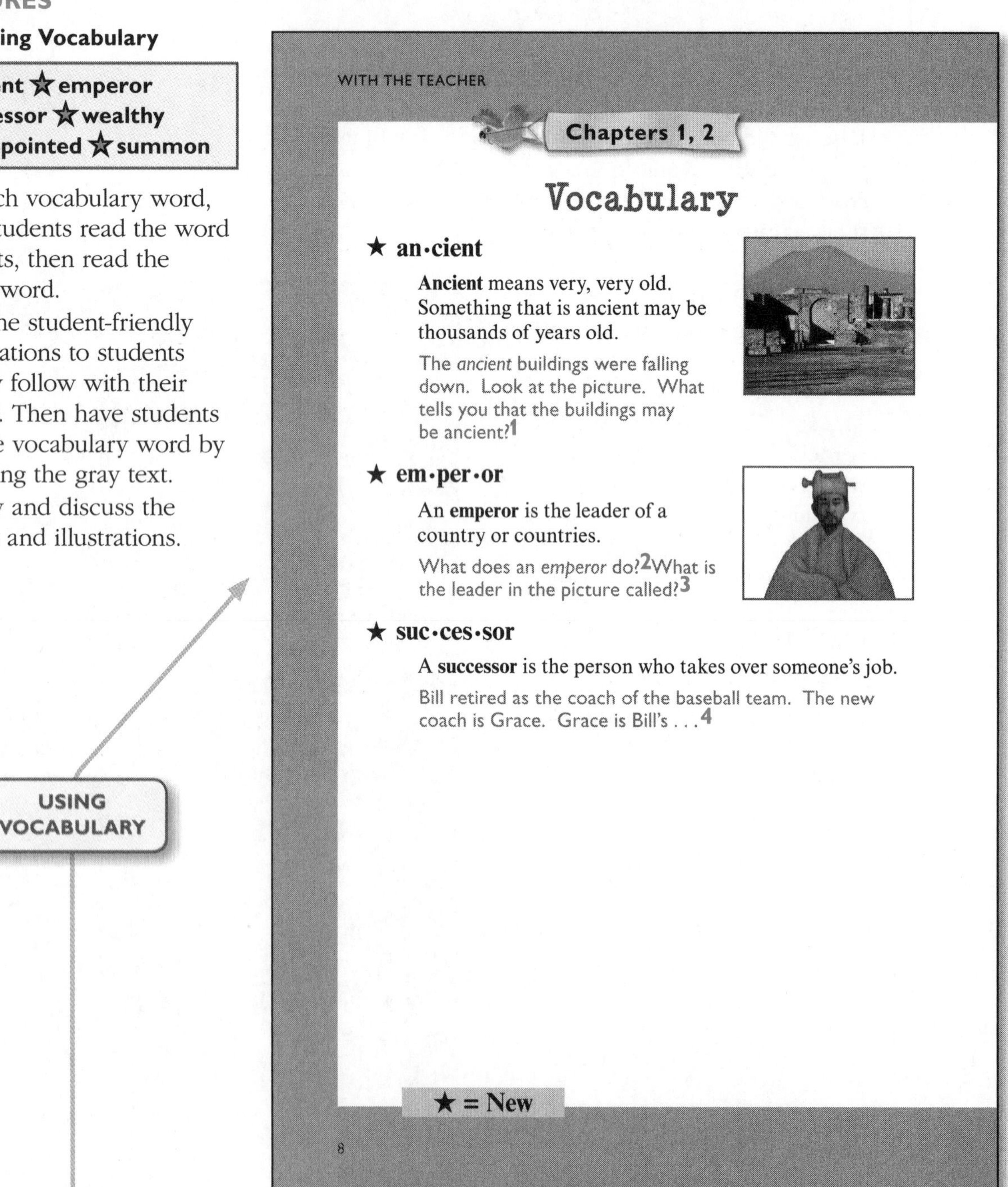
WITH THE TEACHER

Chapters 1, 2

Vocabulary

★ **an•cient**

Ancient means very, very old. Something that is ancient may be thousands of years old.

The *ancient* buildings were falling down. Look at the picture. What tells you that the buildings may be ancient?[1]

★ **em•per•or**

An **emperor** is the leader of a country or countries.

What does an *emperor* do?[2] What is the leader in the picture called?[3]

★ **suc•ces•sor**

A **successor** is the person who takes over someone's job.

Bill retired as the coach of the baseball team. The new coach is Grace. Grace is Bill's . . .[4]

★ = New

8

❶ **Apply:** Explaining; Using Vocabulary—ancient (The buildings may be ancient because they are missing roofs and walls.)

❷ **Remember:** Identifying—What; Using Vocabulary—emperor (An emperor is the leader of a country.)

❸ **Remember:** Identifying—What; Using Vocabulary—emperor (The leader in the picture is an emperor.)

❹ **Understand:** Using Vocabulary—successor (successor)

★= New in this unit

★ **wealth·y**

Wealthy means to have a lot of something—usually money.

A *wealthy* person is someone who has a lot of money. The emperor was . . . 1

★ **dis·ap·point·ed**

Disappointed means to have a feeling of sadness when you don't get what you want.

When they couldn't go on the field trip, the children were sad. What's another way to say "The children were sad because they didn't get what they wanted"? The children were . . . 2

★ **sum·mon**

Summon means to order someone to come to a place.

What's another way to say "The Emperor ordered the people to the palace"? The Emperor . . . 3

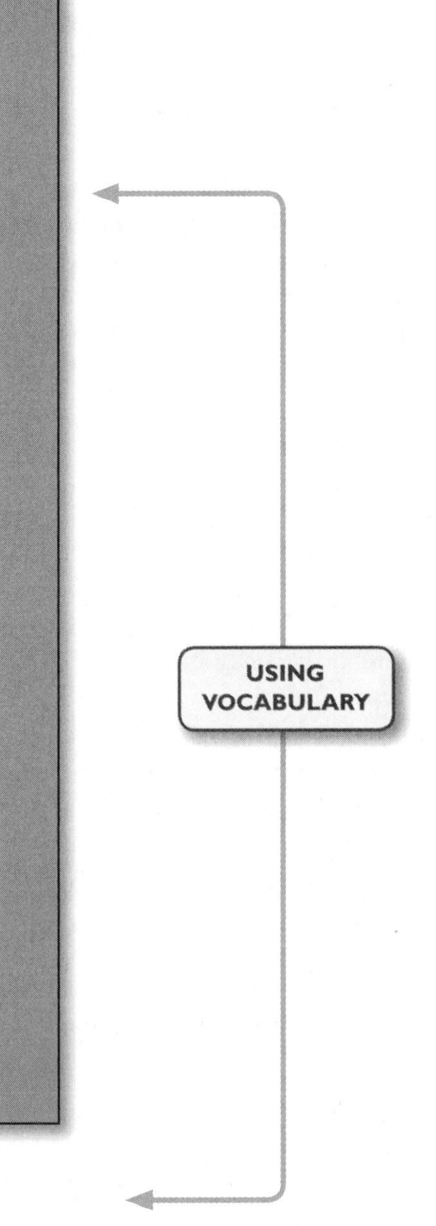

❶ **Understand:** Using Vocabulary—wealthy (wealthy)

❷ **Understand:** Using Vocabulary—disappointed (disappointed)

❸ **Understand:** Using Vocabulary—summoned (summoned the people to the palace)

CHAPTER 1 INSTRUCTIONS

Students read Chapter 1 with the teacher and Chapter 2 on their own.
Note: If you're working on an 8- to 11-Day Plan, you will read Chapter 2 with students.

COMPREHENSION PROCESSES

Remember, Understand, Apply, Analyze

COMPREHENSION BUILDING

- Encourage students to answer questions with complete sentences.
- If students have difficulty comprehending, think aloud with them or reread the portion of the story that answers the question. Repeat the question.

PROCEDURES

1. Introducing Chapter 1

Identifying—Title; Predicting; Defining and Using Vocabulary—emperor
Discuss the title and main character. Say something like:
What's the title of this chapter? (The Emperor)
That's right. The word *emperor* is one of your vocabulary words. What do you think the Emperor in this story does? (He is the leader of a country.)

2. First Reading

- Ask questions and discuss the story as indicated by the gray text.
- Mix group and individual turns, independent of your voice.
  Have students work toward a group accuracy goal of 0–3 errors.
  Quietly keep track of errors made by all students in the group.
- After reading the story, practice any difficult words.
  Reread the story if students have not reached the accuracy goal.

3. Second Reading, Short Passage Practice: Developing Prosody

- Demonstrate expressive, fluent reading of the first paragraph.
  Read at a rate slightly faster than the students' rate. Say something like:
  Listen to my expression as I read the first paragraph.

  "In ancient times, there was a wise and beloved emperor. He ruled the land with fairness and kindness. With no children of his own, the Emperor needed to choose his successor."

- Guide practice with your voice.
  Read the first paragraph with me. In ancient times . . .
- Provide individual turns while others track with their fingers and whisper read.
- Repeat with one paragraph or page at a time. Repeat steps with each remaining paragraph.

CORRECTING DECODING ERRORS

During story reading, gently correct any error, then have students reread the sentence.

REPEATED READINGS

Prosody

On the second reading, students practice developing prosody—phrasing and expression. Research has shown that prosody is related to both fluency and comprehension.

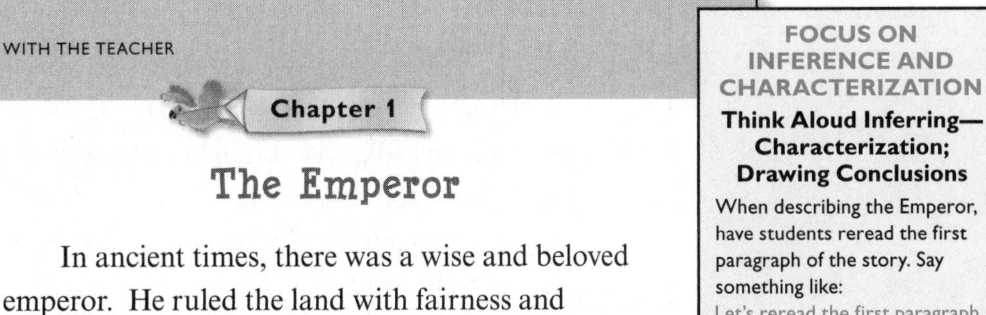

The Emperor

In ancient times, there was a wise and beloved emperor. He ruled the land with fairness and kindness. With no children of his own, the Emperor needed to choose his successor.

Word spread rapidly across the empire. Wealthy parents brought their children from all over the land. Each mother was certain her child would be chosen.

What was the Emperor's goal?[1] Why do you think he was trying to find a *successor*?[2]

10

FOCUS ON INFERENCE AND CHARACTERIZATION

Think Aloud Inferring—Characterization; Drawing Conclusions

When describing the Emperor, have students reread the first paragraph of the story. Say something like:

Let's reread the first paragraph on page 10. Listen to the words that tell about the Emperor. What does it say first? (He was wise.)

That's right. What does that mean? (smart) Yes, it means he was smart. The book doesn't say, but if I read between the lines, that means he made good decisions.

What else does it say in the first sentence? (He was beloved.) What do you think that means? (He was loved . . .) Do you think the people liked the Emperor? (yes) I think he was popular with the people. He was . . . *beloved.*

In the next sentence, it says he ruled with fairness and kindness. What does that mean? (He was fair and kind.)

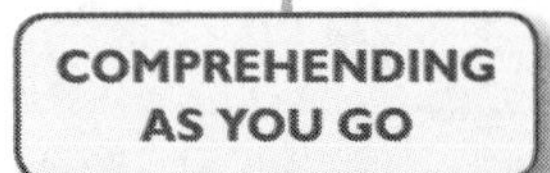

1. **Understand:** Explaining—Goal; Using Vocabulary—successor (The Emperor's goal was to find a successor.)
2. **Apply:** Inferring; Explaining (He didn't have any children. He needed to find someone to take his place . . .)

Hundreds of children, dressed in the finest hand-painted silk, were brought to the Emperor. A line of boys stretched around the palace wall. The Emperor thought for sure he would know when he met the right child.

Day after day, the Emperor thought, "Today is the day. Today is the day that I will meet the next emperor!" But every day he was disappointed.

Why was the Emperor *disappointed?*[1]

COMPREHENDING AS YOU GO

① **Understand:** Explaining; Using Vocabulary—disappointed (The Emperor was disappointed because he could not find a successor.)

★ 4. Introducing Think and Talk

Introduce students to Think and Talk questions. Give students partner numbers (1, 2). Say something like:
We're going to Think and Talk about what we read. Touch Question 1. Read the question. (Who is the main character?)
[Megan], who is the main character? (the Emperor)
Yes, that is correct.

Read question 2. (Describe the Emperor.)
Partner 1, you talk first . . .
Partner 2, your turn to describe the Emperor . . .

[Sam], how did you and your partner describe the Emperor? (He is kind.)
Great. What else can we say about the Emperor? (He is fair.)

Continue with the rest of the questions. Use partners, as appropriate. (See Important Tips on page 11 for an elaborated script.)

Note: Time will dictate how deeply you can engage students in Think and Talk.

WITH THE TEACHER

The Emperor walked in the quiet of his garden. He thought to himself, "The boys wear the finest silks. They are from the best of families. They all show me the greatest respect, but they all seem the same. What shall I do?"

The Emperor could hear the hum of the bees. The graceful plum blossoms fluttered in the gentle wind. They almost seemed to whisper. Finally, in the peace of his garden, the Emperor knew what he would do.

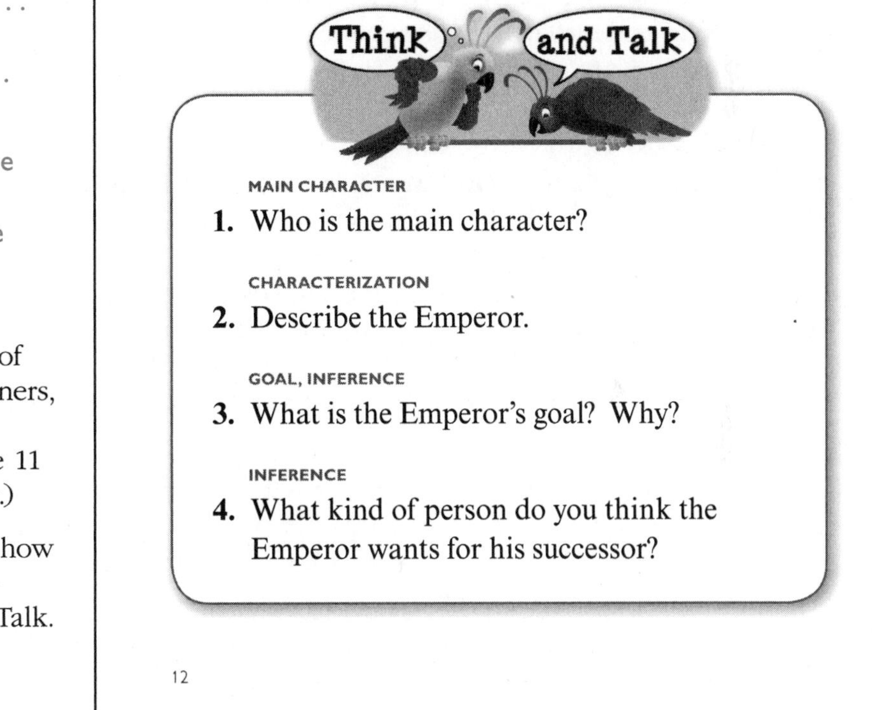

MAIN CHARACTER
1. Who is the main character?

CHARACTERIZATION
2. Describe the Emperor.

GOAL, INFERENCE
3. What is the Emperor's goal? Why?

INFERENCE
4. What kind of person do you think the Emperor wants for his successor?

12

❶ **Remember:** Identifying—Main Character (The main character is the Emperor.)

❷ **Understand:** Describing (He is kind, beloved, popular, fair, wise, a good leader . . .)

❸ **Remember:** Identifying—Goal; **Understand:** Inferring, Explaining (He wants and needs a successor. He has no children.)

❹ **Apply:** Inferring (He probably wants someone like himself—someone who is fair, kind, and wise.)

★ = New in this unit

CHAPTER 2 INSTRUCTIONS

Students read without the teacher, independently or with partners.
Note: If you're working on an 8- to 11-Day Plan, you will read Chapter 2 with students.

COMPREHENSION PROCESSES

Understand, Apply, Analyze

PROCEDURES FOR READING ON YOUR OWN

1. Getting Ready
Have students turn to Chapter 2 on page 13.

> **PREP NOTE**
> **Setting a Purpose**
> Write questions on a chalkboard, white board, or large piece of paper before working with your small group.

2. Setting a Purpose

Explaining, Identifying—Main Character
Before students begin reading, say something like:
In the next pages, you are going to find out about the Emperor's plan.
Read to find out the answers to these questions:
- What did the Emperor give to each boy?
- What did he tell the boys to do?
- Who is Jun?

3. Reading on Your Own: Partner or Whisper Reading
- Have students take turns reading every other page with a partner, or have students whisper read pages 13–15 on their own.
- Continue having students track each word with their fingers.
  Note: Finger tracking allows you to monitor student engagement and helps students increase accuracy and fluency.
- Have students ask themselves or their partners the gray text questions.

For Whisper Reading, say something like:
Everyone, turn to page 13. This is where you're going to start reading on your own—without me. You will whisper read as you track with your finger, so I can see where you are in your work.
Turn to page 15. That's where you are going to stop reading.
Now turn back to page 13.

For Partner Reading, say something like:
Everyone, turn to page 13. This is where you're going to start Partner Reading.
Where are you going to sit? (at our desks, side by side)
You will take turns reading pages. If you are the listener, what will you do? (keep my book flat, follow with my finger, compliment my partner)
If you are the reader, what will you do? (keep my book flat, finger track, read quietly)
Turn to page 15. That's where you are going to stop reading.

4. Comprehension and Skill Work
For students on a 7-Day Plan, tell them they will do Comprehension and Skill Activities 1 and 2 after they read Chapter 2 on their own. Guide practice, as needed. For teacher directions, see pages 30 and 31. (For 8- to 11-Day Plans, see the Lesson Planner, page 9.)

5. Homework 1: Repeated Reading

Chapter 2

The Seed

Again, the children were summoned to the palace. A long line of boys formed around the palace wall. One by one, the boys entered the palace. One by one, the boys in their fine silks were given a small seed. Each boy was told to plant the seed and bring it back in the spring. Each boy placed his seed in a small silk bag.

What do you think the Emperor wants the boys to do?[1] How do you think he will choose the next emperor?[2]

COMPREHENDING AS YOU GO

1. **Understand:** Explaining (He wants them to plant the seeds and bring them back in the spring.)
2. **Apply:** Inferring, Predicting (He will see who can grow the biggest plant. He will choose the boy who takes the best care of his seed . . .)

ON YOUR OWN

Finally, all the young boys had taken their seeds home. One seed remained. The Emperor returned to his garden. There, an old gardener and his grandson were pruning the plum tree. The grandfather held his grandson's hand and showed him how to make the cuts. Snip. Snip. The little boy's dark eyes danced with happiness.

Why do you think the boy was happy?[1]

14

COMPREHENDING AS YOU GO

❶ **Apply:** Inferring, Making Connections (The boy was happy because he was working with his grandfather. The boy was happy because he got to prune the tree . . .)

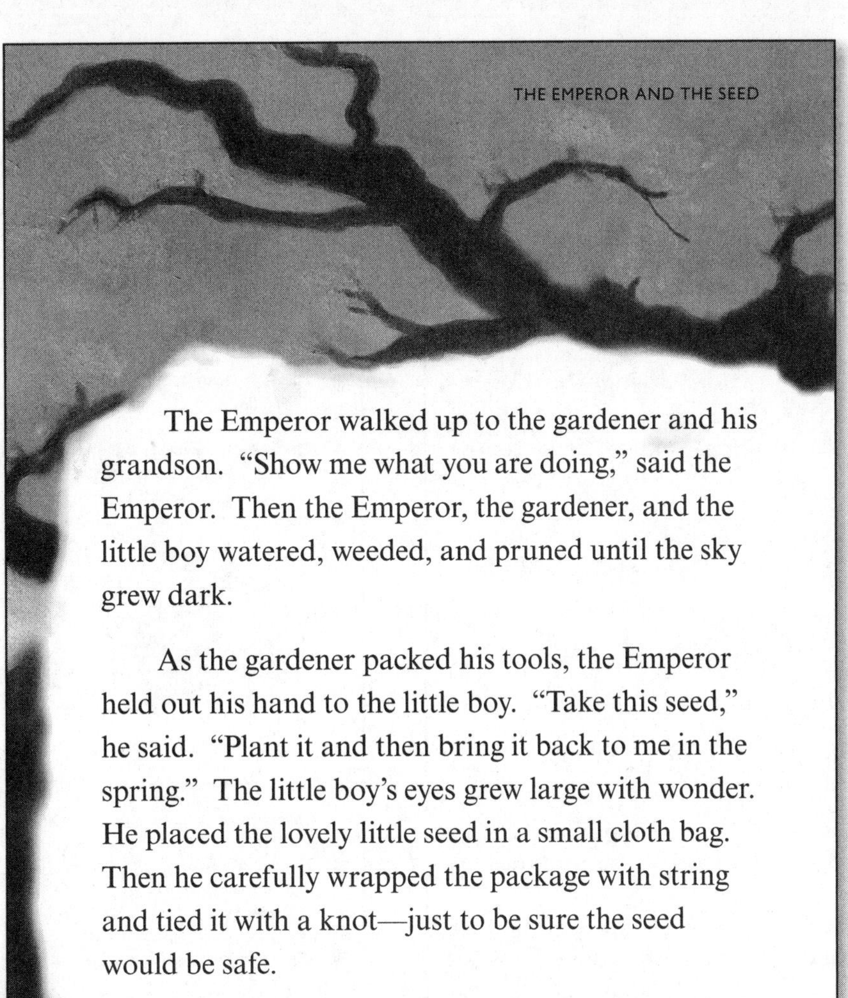

The Emperor walked up to the gardener and his grandson. "Show me what you are doing," said the Emperor. Then the Emperor, the gardener, and the little boy watered, weeded, and pruned until the sky grew dark.

As the gardener packed his tools, the Emperor held out his hand to the little boy. "Take this seed," he said. "Plant it and then bring it back to me in the spring." The little boy's eyes grew large with wonder. He placed the lovely little seed in a small cloth bag. Then he carefully wrapped the package with string and tied it with a knot—just to be sure the seed would be safe.

As the boy and his grandfather left the garden, the Emperor said, "What is your name?"

The small boy said, "My name is Jun (Jen)."

What do you think the boy will do with the seed?[1] How can you tell the boy will take good care of his seed?[2] What is Jun's goal?[3]

COMPREHENDING AS YOU GO

1. **Apply:** Inferring (He will plant the seed and take good care of it.)
2. **Apply:** Inferring, Explaining (He wrapped it carefully so it would be safe.)
3. **Understand:** Explaining—Goal (His goal is to plant the seed and take good care of it so he can bring it back in the spring.)

STORY COMPREHENSION

COMPREHENSION PROCESSES

Remember, Understand, Evaluate

WRITING TRAITS

Conventions—Capital, Period

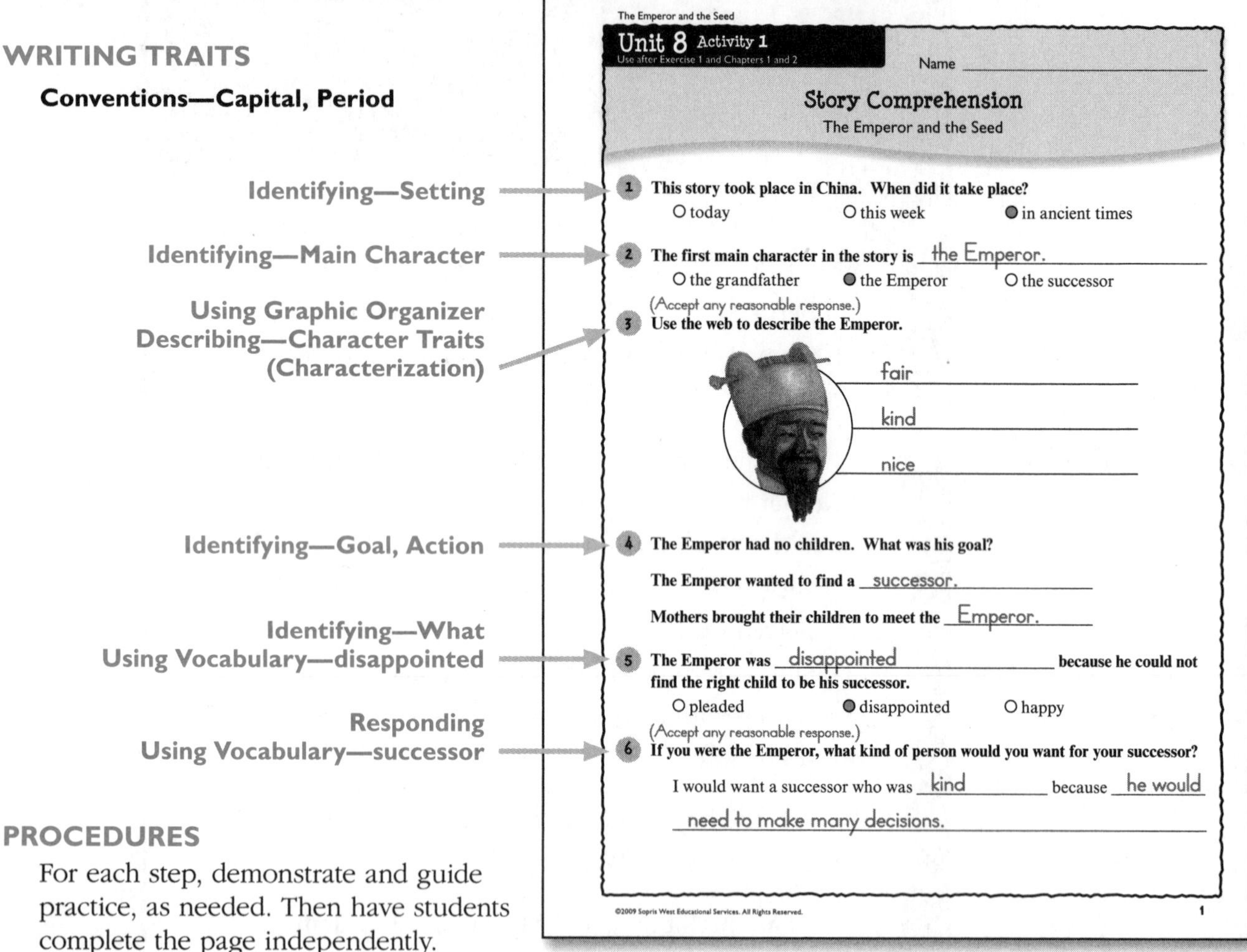

The Emperor and the Seed

Unit 8 Activity 1
Use after Exercise 1 and Chapters 1 and 2

Name ____________

Story Comprehension
The Emperor and the Seed

1. This story took place in China. When did it take place?
 ○ today ○ this week ● in ancient times

2. The first main character in the story is the Emperor.
 ○ the grandfather ● the Emperor ○ the successor

(Accept any reasonable response.)
3. Use the web to describe the Emperor.
 fair
 kind
 nice

4. The Emperor had no children. What was his goal?
 The Emperor wanted to find a successor.
 Mothers brought their children to meet the Emperor.

5. The Emperor was disappointed because he could not find the right child to be his successor.
 ○ pleaded ● disappointed ○ happy

(Accept any reasonable response.)
6. If you were the Emperor, what kind of person would you want for your successor?
 I would want a successor who was kind because he would need to make many decisions.

©2009 Sopris West Educational Services. All Rights Reserved. 1

PROCEDURES

For each step, demonstrate and guide practice, as needed. Then have students complete the page independently.

1. **Selection Response** (Items 1, 2, 5)

2. **Characterization: Web—Specific Instructions** (Item 3)
   Have students write descriptions of the Emperor in the blanks.

3. **Sentence Completion—Specific Instructions** (Item 4)
   - Have students read the sentence, questions, and sentence stems.
     Say something like:
     Read the sentence for Item 4. (The Emperor had no children.)
     Read the question. (What was his goal?)
     Read and complete the sentence. (The Emperor wanted to find a . . . successor.)
   - Have students write answers that correctly complete the sentences.

4. **Personal Response: Sentence Completion—Specific Instructions** (Item 6)
   - Have students read the item, then brainstorm possible responses. If students have difficulty, demonstrate an appropriate response. I would want a successor who was honest because . . . I would want a successor who was fair because . . .
   - Have students write their own responses.

★VISUALIZING AND ILLUSTRATING

COMPREHENSION PROCESSES

Understand

WRITING TRAITS

Conventions—Period

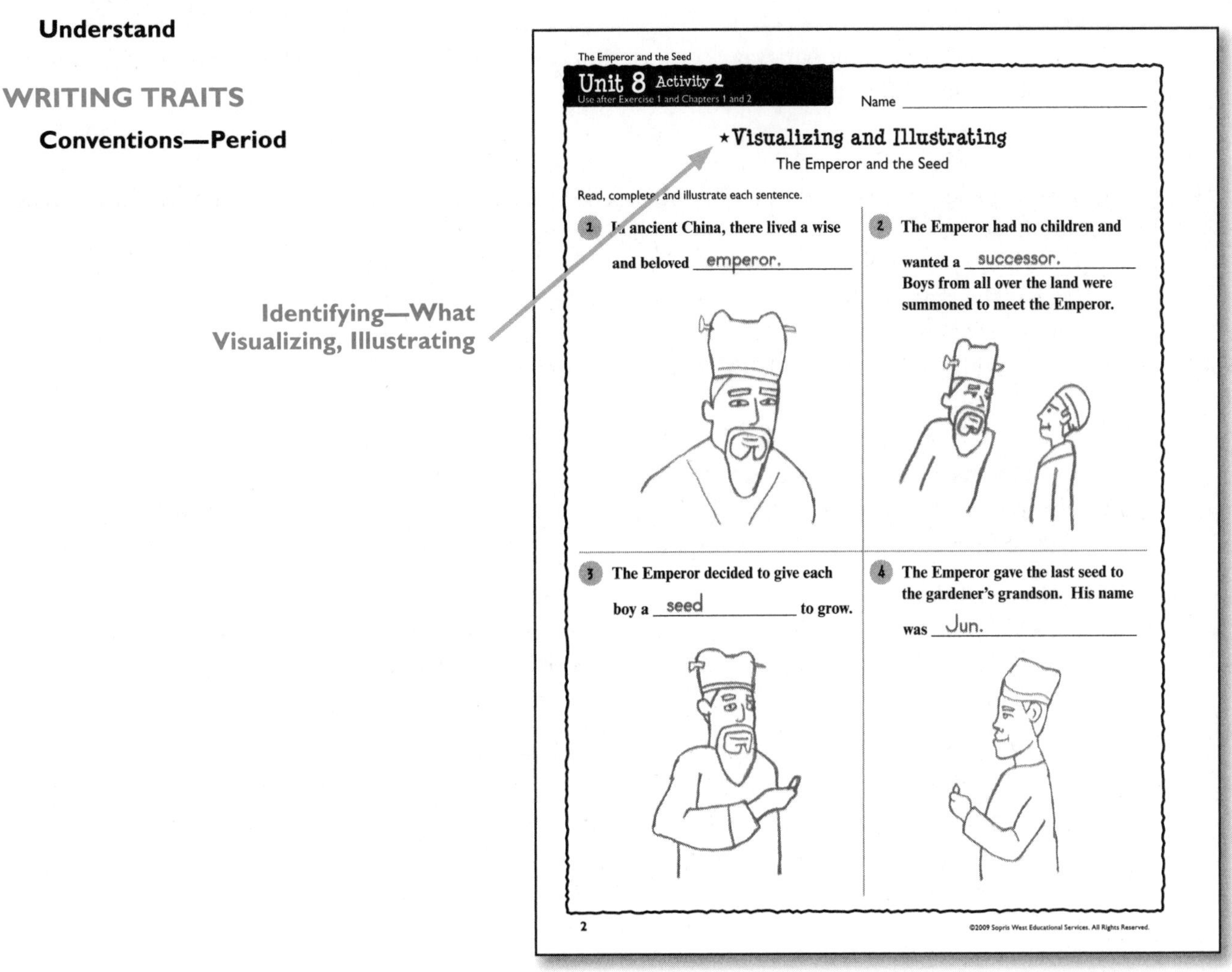

The Emperor and the Seed

Unit 8 Activity 2
Use after Exercise 1 and Chapters 1 and 2

Name ___________

★Visualizing and Illustrating

The Emperor and the Seed

Read, complete, and illustrate each sentence.

1. In ancient China, there lived a wise and beloved emperor.
2. The Emperor had no children and wanted a successor. Boys from all over the land were summoned to meet the Emperor.
3. The Emperor decided to give each boy a seed to grow.
4. The Emperor gave the last seed to the gardener's grandson. His name was Jun.

2

PROCEDURES

For each step, demonstrate and guide practice, as needed. Then have students complete the page independently.

★ **Sentence Completion, Illustrating—Introductory Instructions** (Items 1–4)

- Have students read, complete, and illustrate each sentence. Encourage students to visualize what they will draw in each box and to include as many details as possible. Say something like:
  To illustrate the sentences in each box, you can first imagine, or visualize, what the sentences describe. Remember, visualizing helps you understand what you are reading. This is what we did in today's Focus Lesson. Read and complete the first sentence stem. (In ancient China, there lived a wise and beloved . . . emperor.)
  To illustrate that sentence, I can imagine the Emperor standing in his palace garden.
  Can you imagine what he is wearing? (a colorful robe, a Chinese hat . . .)
  What else could be in the picture? (beautiful flowers in the garden, a palace wall . . .)
  Yes, those details will make your illustrations just great! When you start drawing, you may want to look in your book for more ideas.
- Remind students to end each sentence with a period.

★= New in this unit

❶ SOUND REVIEW

Have students read the sounds and key word phrases. Work for accuracy, then fluency.

❷ SHIFTY WORD BLENDING

For each word, have students say the underlined sound. Then have them sound out the word smoothly and say it. Use the words in sentences, as appropriate.

❸ SOUND PRACTICE

- For each task, have students spell and say the focus sound in the gray bar. For Buildups, read the header.
  Next, have students read each underlined sound two times, then the word.
  Look at the gray bar. Say k-n says /nnn/ as in knee. (K-n says /nnn/ as in knee.)
  Read each sound two times. Then say the word. /nnn/, /nnn/, know, /nnn/, /nnn/ knew . . .)
- Repeat with each column, building accuracy first, then fluency.

❹ ACCURACY AND FLUENCY BUILDING

- For each task, have students say any underlined part, then read the word.
- Set a pace. Then have students read the whole words in each task and column.
- Provide repeated practice, building accuracy first, then fluency.

C1. Multisyllabic Words

- For the list of words divided by syllables, have students read and finger count each syllable, then read the word. Use the word in a sentence, as appropriate.
- For the list of whole words, build accuracy and then fluency.

empty	2 syllables	There was nothing in the cookie jar. It was . . . *empty.*
despite	2 syllables	I hurt my ankle. I played soccer . . . *despite* . . . my sore ankle.
embarrassed	3 syllables	When Eiko tripped in the cafeteria, she felt . . . *embarrassed.*
integrity	4 syllables	Zeke is honest. He has . . . *integrity.*
surprise	2 syllables	I asked what my present was, but Mom said it was a . . . *surprise.*

D1. Tricky Words

- For each Tricky Word, have students use the sounds and word parts they know to silently sound out the word. Use the word in a sentence to help with pronunciation.
- If the word is unfamiliar, tell students the word. Then have students say, spell, and say it.

lie

Look at the first word. This word rhymes with *tie* and *die*. Read the word. (lie) Spell it. (l-i-e)
Someone who is honest doesn't . . . *lie.* Read the word three times. (lie, lie, lie)

clothes	The princess had many beautiful . . . *clothes.*
brought	Ned asked, "Did you bring a present?" Amanda said, "Yes, I . . . *brought* . . . one."
beautiful	The princess was very . . . *beautiful.*
taught	Jun learned many things from his grandfather. His grandfather . . . *taught* . . . Jun.

❺ WORDS IN CONTEXT

For each word, have students use the sounds and word parts they know to silently sound out the word. Then have students read the sentence. Assist, as needed.

6 AFFIXES

★Have students practice reading *-able* and the related words. Use each word in a sentence.

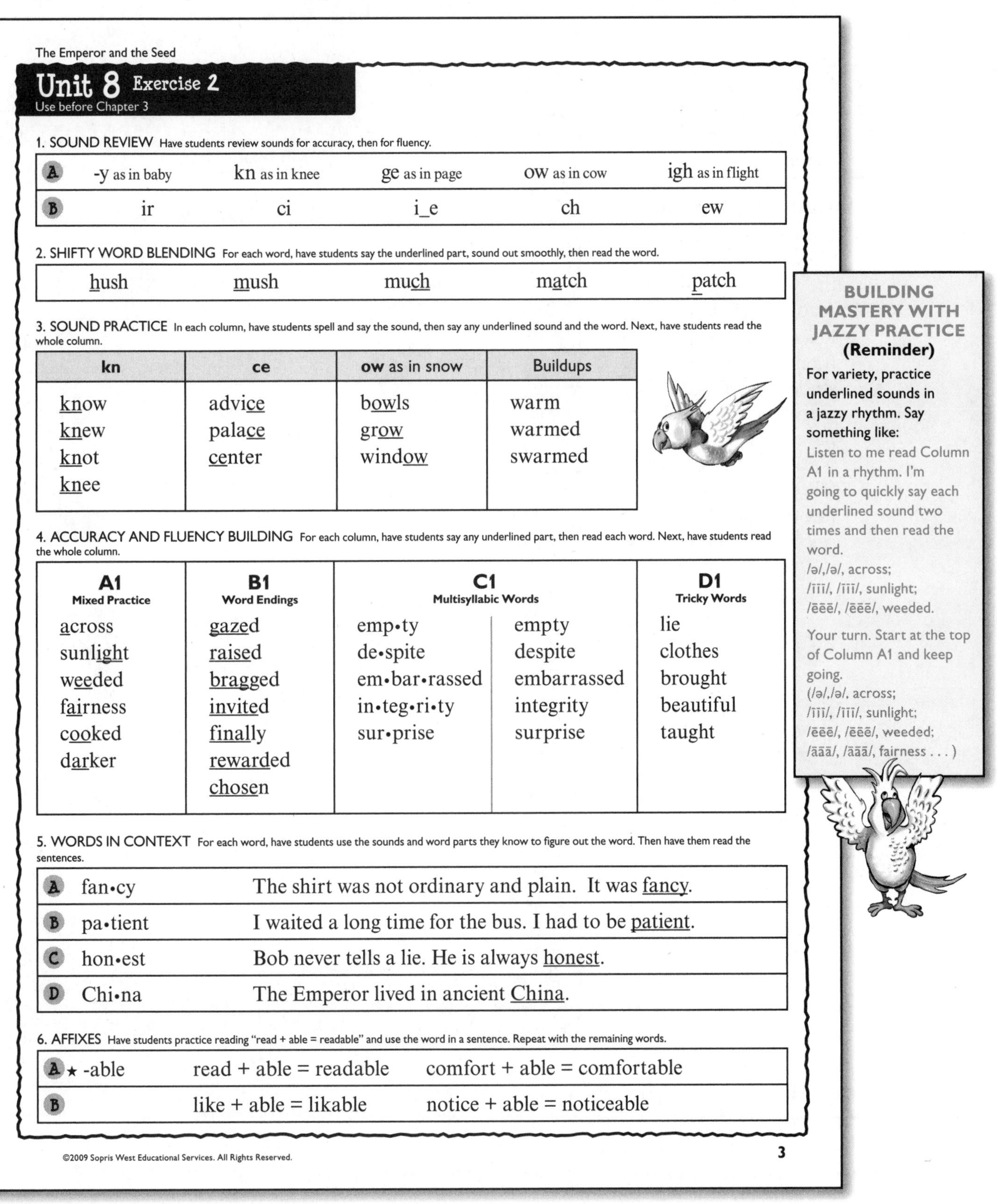

The Emperor and the Seed

Unit 8 Exercise 2
Use before Chapter 3

1. SOUND REVIEW Have students review sounds for accuracy, then for fluency.

A	-y as in baby	kn as in knee	ge as in page	ow as in cow	igh as in flight
B	ir	ci	i_e	ch	ew

2. SHIFTY WORD BLENDING For each word, have students say the underlined part, sound out smoothly, then read the word.

hush	mush	much	match	patch

3. SOUND PRACTICE In each column, have students spell and say the sound, then say any underlined sound and the word. Next, have students read the whole column.

kn	ce	ow as in snow	Buildups
know	advice	bowls	warm
knew	palace	grow	warmed
knot	center	window	swarmed
knee			

4. ACCURACY AND FLUENCY BUILDING For each column, have students say any underlined part, then read each word. Next, have students read the whole column.

A1 Mixed Practice	B1 Word Endings	C1 Multisyllabic Words		D1 Tricky Words
across	gazed	emp•ty	empty	lie
sunlight	raised	de•spite	despite	clothes
weeded	bragged	em•bar•rassed	embarrassed	brought
fairness	invited	in•teg•ri•ty	integrity	beautiful
cooked	finally	sur•prise	surprise	taught
darker	rewarded			
	chosen			

5. WORDS IN CONTEXT For each word, have students use the sounds and word parts they know to figure out the word. Then have them read the sentences.

A	fan•cy	The shirt was not ordinary and plain. It was fancy.
B	pa•tient	I waited a long time for the bus. I had to be patient.
C	hon•est	Bob never tells a lie. He is always honest.
D	Chi•na	The Emperor lived in ancient China.

6. AFFIXES Have students practice reading "read + able = readable" and use the word in a sentence. Repeat with the remaining words.

A	★ -able	read + able = readable	comfort + able = comfortable
B		like + able = likable	notice + able = noticeable

BUILDING MASTERY WITH JAZZY PRACTICE (Reminder)

For variety, practice underlined sounds in a jazzy rhythm. Say something like:

Listen to me read Column A1 in a rhythm. I'm going to quickly say each underlined sound two times and then read the word. /ə/,/ə/, across; /īīī/, /īīī/, sunlight; /ēēē/, /ēēē/, weeded.

Your turn. Start at the top of Column A1 and keep going. (/ə/,/ə/, across; /īīī/, /īīī/, sunlight; /ēēē/, /ēēē/, weeded; /āāā/, /āāā/, fairness . . .)

★= New in this unit

COMPREHENSION PROCESSES

Understand, Apply

PROCEDURES

★ **advice** ★ **brag**
★ **embarrassed** ★ **despite**
★ **integrity, ancient, successor**

1. Introducing Vocabulary

- For each vocabulary word, have students read the word by parts, then read the whole word.
- Read the student-friendly explanations to students as they follow with their fingers. Then have students use the vocabulary word by following the gray text.
- Review and discuss the photos and illustrations.

USING VOCABULARY

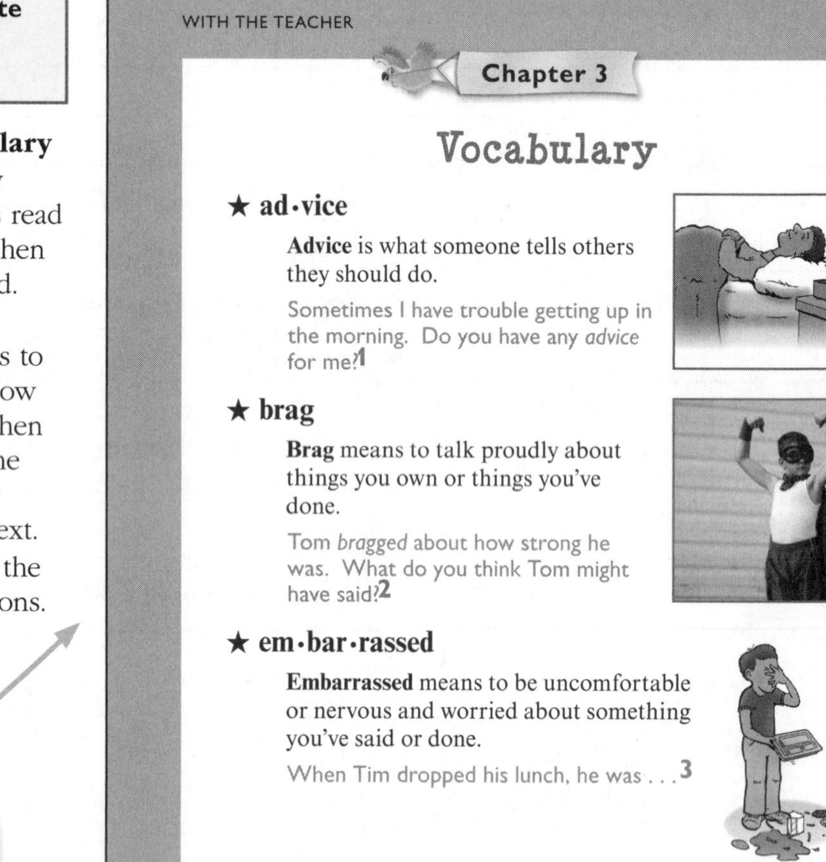

WITH THE TEACHER

Chapter 3

Vocabulary

★ **ad•vice**

Advice is what someone tells others they should do.

Sometimes I have trouble getting up in the morning. Do you have any *advice* for me?1

★ **brag**

Brag means to talk proudly about things you own or things you've done.

Tom *bragged* about how strong he was. What do you think Tom might have said?2

★ **em•bar•rassed**

Embarrassed means to be uncomfortable or nervous and worried about something you've said or done.

When Tim dropped his lunch, he was . . . 3

★ = New

16

❶ **Apply:** Using Vocabulary—advice (My advice is to go to bed earlier. My advice is to have someone wake you up . . .)

❷ **Understand:** Defining Vocabulary—brag (I am really strong. I can lift up my big brother . . .)

❸ **Understand:** Using Vocabulary—embarrassed (embarrassed)

★ = New in this unit

2. Now You Try It!

- Read or paraphrase the directions.
- Then, for each word, have students read the word by parts and then read the whole word.
- Have students explain or define the word in their own words. Say something like:

  Look at the first word. Say the parts, then read the whole word. (an•cient, ancient)

  Now, let's pretend that we're going to explain or define the word *ancient* to a friend. [Randy], what would you say? Start with "*Ancient* means . . ." (Ancient means very, very old.)

  That's right. Something that is ancient is very, very old. [Marlie], when something is ancient, how many years old is it? (Something ancient might be hundreds or thousands of years old.)
- Have students turn to the appropriate page in the glossary and discuss how their definitions are the same as or different from those in the glossary. Your students may like their definitions better.

Note: By defining a word in their own words, students are demonstrating depth of word knowledge. Verbatim responses only demonstrate memorization. Encourage paraphrasing.

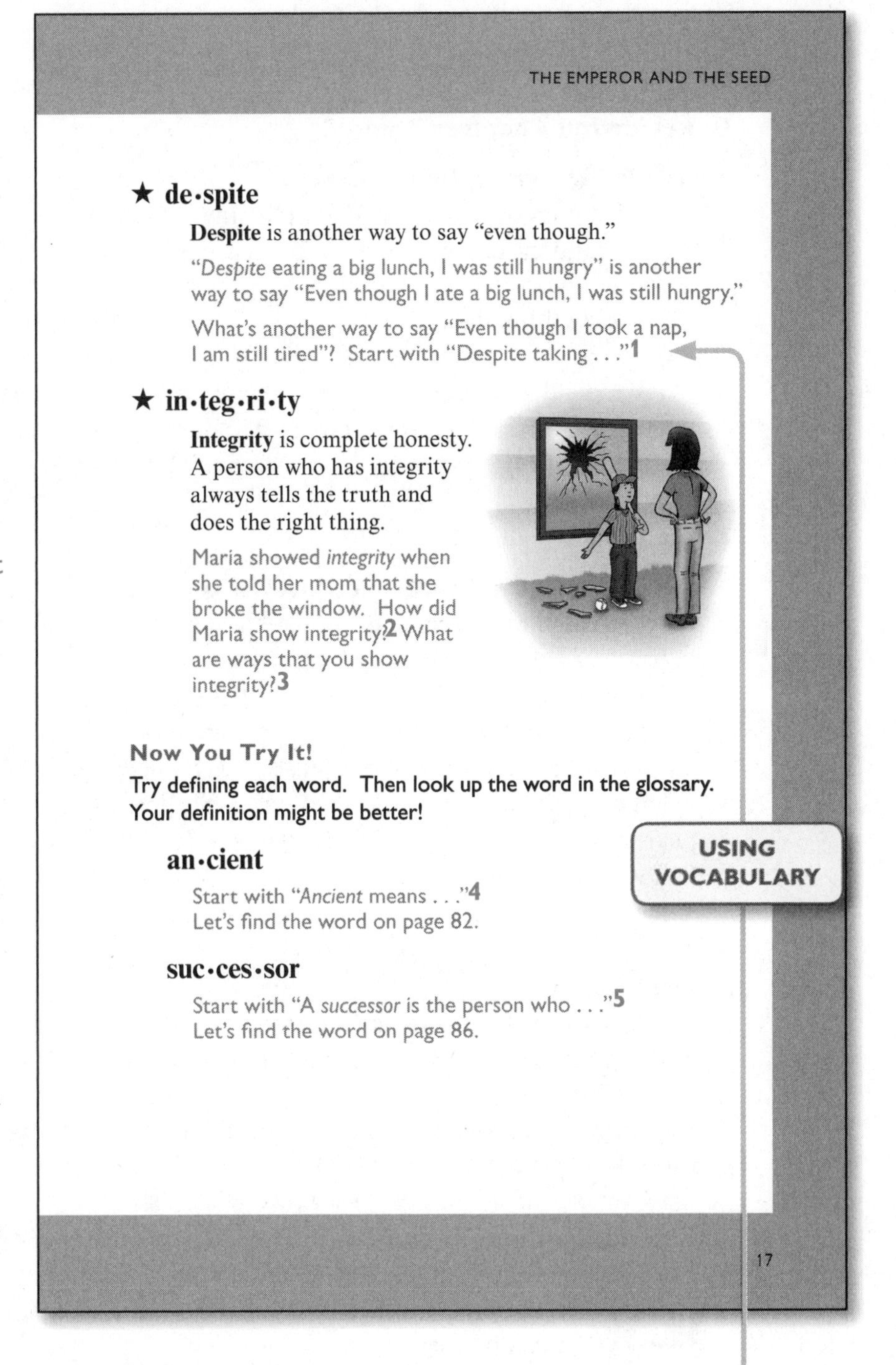
THE EMPEROR AND THE SEED

★ **de•spite**

Despite is another way to say "even though."

"*Despite* eating a big lunch, I was still hungry" is another way to say "Even though I ate a big lunch, I was still hungry."

What's another way to say "Even though I took a nap, I am still tired"? Start with "Despite taking . . ."1

★ **in•teg•ri•ty**

Integrity is complete honesty. A person who has integrity always tells the truth and does the right thing.

Maria showed *integrity* when she told her mom that she broke the window. How did Maria show integrity?2 What are ways that you show integrity?3

Now You Try It!

Try defining each word. Then look up the word in the glossary. Your definition might be better!

an•cient

Start with "*Ancient* means . . ."4
Let's find the word on page 82.

suc•ces•sor

Start with "A *successor* is the person who . . ."5
Let's find the word on page 86.

USING VOCABULARY

17

❶ **Understand:** Using Vocabulary—despite (Despite taking a nap, I was still tired.)

❷ **Understand:** Using Vocabulary—integrity (Maria showed integrity when she told her mom that she broke the window.)

❸ **Understand:** Defining Vocabulary—integrity (I show integrity when . . .)

❹ **Understand:** Defining Vocabulary—ancient (Ancient means very, very old . . .)

❺ **Understand:** Defining Vocabulary—successor (A successor is the person who takes over someone's job . . .)

CHAPTER 3 INSTRUCTIONS

Students read Chapter 3 with the teacher.

COMPREHENSION PROCESSES

Remember, Understand, Apply, Analyze

PROCEDURES

1. Reviewing Chapters 1 and 2

Identifying—What, Main Character

- Have students turn to page 10. Quickly review the Emperor's character and goal.
- Have student turn to page 13. If time permits, have students reread Chapter 2 with you. Quickly discuss the questions on the board from Chapter 2, Setting a Purpose. Say something like:

  Let's see what you found out about the Emperor's plan to find a successor.
  What did the Emperor give to each boy? (He gave them each a small seed.)
  What did he tell the boys to do? (He told them to plant the seed and bring it back in the spring.)
  Who is Jun? (Jun is the gardener's grandson. The Emperor gave him the last seed to plant.)

2. Introducing Chapter 3

Identifying—Title, What; Inferring; Using Vocabulary—successor; Predicting

Discuss the title. Say something like:

What's the title of this chapter? (The Successor)
Why do you think this chapter is called "The Successor"? (We will find out who the Emperor picks as his successor, who the Emperor picks to take over for him . . .)
Look at the picture on page 19. What is Jun doing? (He is looking at his pot.)
What do you think will happen to Jun's seed? (It will grow into a beautiful plant . . .)
Jun is an interesting name. In China, *Jun* is a word that means *truth.*
Who do you think will become the next emperor? (Maybe it will be Jun.)
Why? (He is a main character. He is nice . . .)

3. First Reading

- Ask questions and discuss the story as indicated by the gray text.
- Mix group and individual turns. Have students work toward a group accuracy goal of 0–5 errors.
- After reading the story, practice any difficult words. Reread the story if students have not reached the accuracy goal.

4. Second Reading, Timed Readings: Repeated Reading

- As time allows, have students do Timed Readings while others follow along.
- Time individuals for 30 seconds and encourage each child to work for a personal best.

5. Partner or Whisper Reading: Repeated Reading

Before beginning independent work, have students finger track and partner or whisper read.

6. Comprehension and Skill Work

Tell students they will do Comprehension and Skill Activities 3 and 4 after they read Chapter 3. Guide practice, as needed. (For teacher directions, see pages 41 and 42.)

7. Homework 2: Repeated Reading

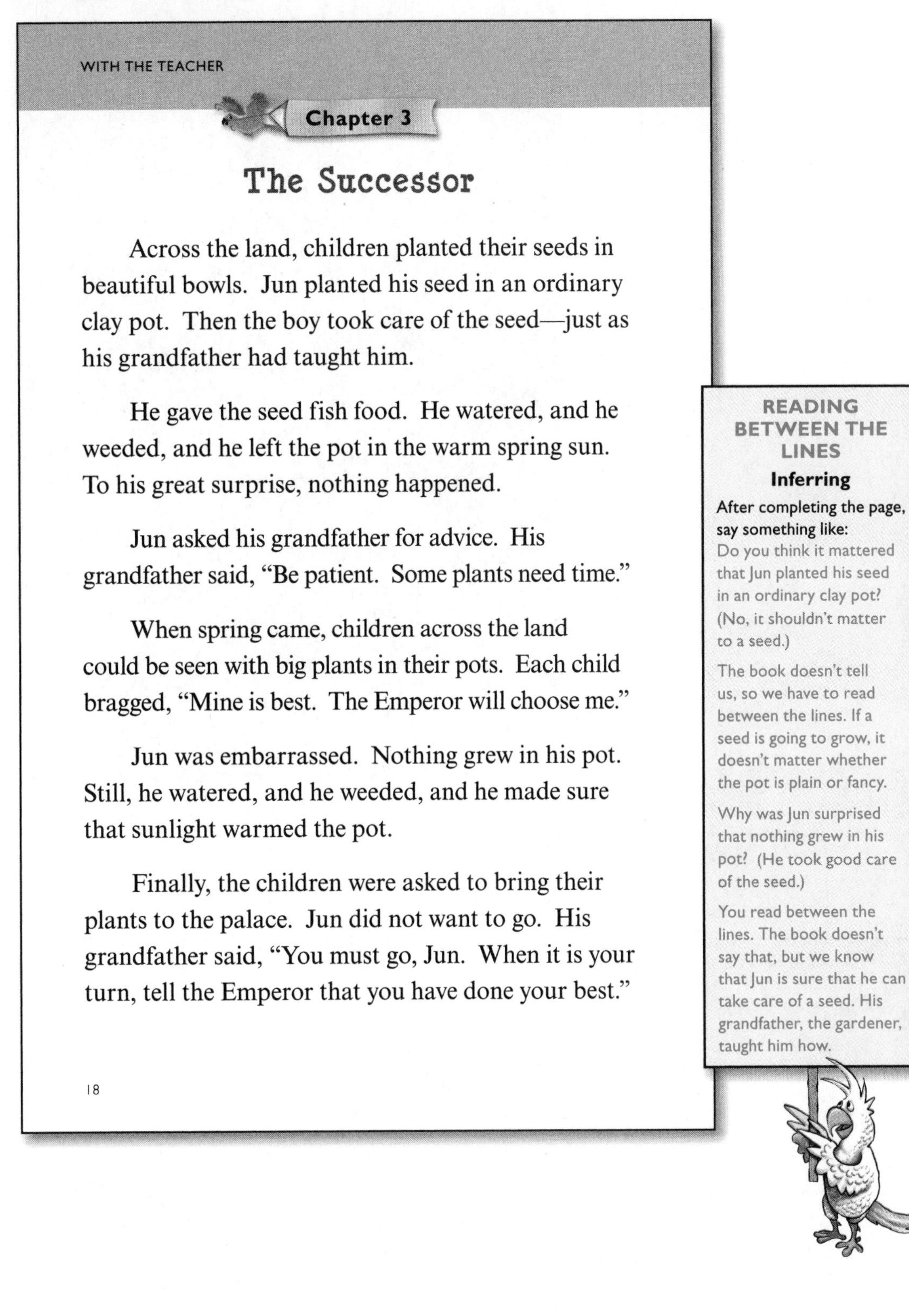

WITH THE TEACHER

Chapter 3

The Successor

Across the land, children planted their seeds in beautiful bowls. Jun planted his seed in an ordinary clay pot. Then the boy took care of the seed—just as his grandfather had taught him.

He gave the seed fish food. He watered, and he weeded, and he left the pot in the warm spring sun. To his great surprise, nothing happened.

Jun asked his grandfather for advice. His grandfather said, "Be patient. Some plants need time."

When spring came, children across the land could be seen with big plants in their pots. Each child bragged, "Mine is best. The Emperor will choose me."

Jun was embarrassed. Nothing grew in his pot. Still, he watered, and he weeded, and he made sure that sunlight warmed the pot.

Finally, the children were asked to bring their plants to the palace. Jun did not want to go. His grandfather said, "You must go, Jun. When it is your turn, tell the Emperor that you have done your best."

18

READING BETWEEN THE LINES

Inferring

After completing the page, say something like:

Do you think it mattered that Jun planted his seed in an ordinary clay pot? (No, it shouldn't matter to a seed.)

The book doesn't tell us, so we have to read between the lines. If a seed is going to grow, it doesn't matter whether the pot is plain or fancy.

Why was Jun surprised that nothing grew in his pot? (He took good care of the seed.)

You read between the lines. The book doesn't say that, but we know that Jun is sure that he can take care of a seed. His grandfather, the gardener, taught him how.

THE EMPEROR AND THE SEED

Who is this part of the story about?[1] What is Jun's problem?[2] Why is Jun *embarrassed*?[3] What was his grandfather's *advice*?[4]

19

COMPREHENDING AS YOU GO

❶ **Remember:** Identifying—Main Character (This part of the story is about Jun.)

❷ **Understand:** Explaining—Problem (Jun's problem is that he can't get his seed to grow.)

❸ **Understand:** Explaining; Using Vocabulary—embarrassed (Jun is embarrassed because nothing grew in his pot.)

❹ **Remember:** Identifying—What; Using Vocabulary—advice (His grandfather's advice was to be patient because some plants need time.)

Jun stood in line at the palace wall. The other children made fun of his plain clothes and empty pot. The little boy's dark eyes grew darker, but he did not say a word.

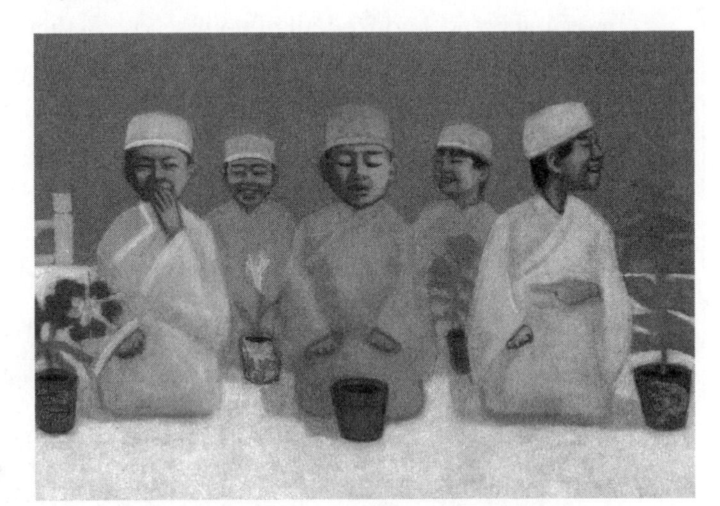

Finally, the Emperor invited all the children into the palace. The Emperor gazed at the fancy bowls, the huge plants, and the colorful blossoms. "Ah, they are quite beautiful," said the Emperor.

Then, to everyone's surprise, the Emperor asked Jun and his grandfather to come sit near him. A hush fell over the room.

A hush fell over the room. What do you think that means?[1] Why do you think that happened?[2]

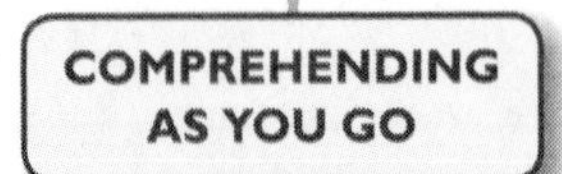

1. **Apply:** Inferring (It means everyone stopped talking. It became very quiet . . .)
2. **Apply:** Inferring; Explaining (Everyone was quiet because they wanted to hear what the Emperor said to Jun. They were surprised that the Emperor wanted to see Jun . . .)

The Emperor said, "The gardener has raised his grandson well. Like each of you, Jun was given one seed. He watered the seed and weeded around it. He made sure the sun warmed the seed. Despite his care, nothing grew. I cooked all of your seeds, so they could not grow. When Jun's seed did not grow, he did not lie. He was honest and brought me his empty pot."

"Jun will grow into a man of great integrity," the Emperor said. "He will treat you with fairness and honesty. One day, Jun will be Emperor of all China."

Why did the other boys disappoint the Emperor?[1] How did Jun show that he had *integrity*?[2] Why did the Emperor choose Jun to be his successor?[3]

21

LESSON

Explaining—Lesson

After completing the page, say something like:
What important lesson does this story teach?

Note: There are many acceptable ways to state the lesson. Paraphrase student responses.

NOTE

Students will complete the Character Comparison Matrix on storybook page 22 in Story Reading 3.

COMPREHENDING AS YOU GO

1. **Analyze:** Drawing Conclusions; **Apply:** Using Vocabulary—disappointed (The boys disappointed the Emperor because they weren't honest. They pretended to grow plants when their seeds didn't sprout.)
2. **Apply:** Explaining; Using Vocabulary—integrity (Jun showed integrity by bringing his empty pot back to the Emperor.)
3. **Understand:** Explaining; Using Vocabulary—successor, integrity (The Emperor chose Jun to be his successor because Jun had integrity.)

CHARACTERIZATION AND VOCABULARY

COMPREHENSION PROCESSES

Apply, Analyze

Inferring; Drawing Conclusions
Using Vocabulary—integrity

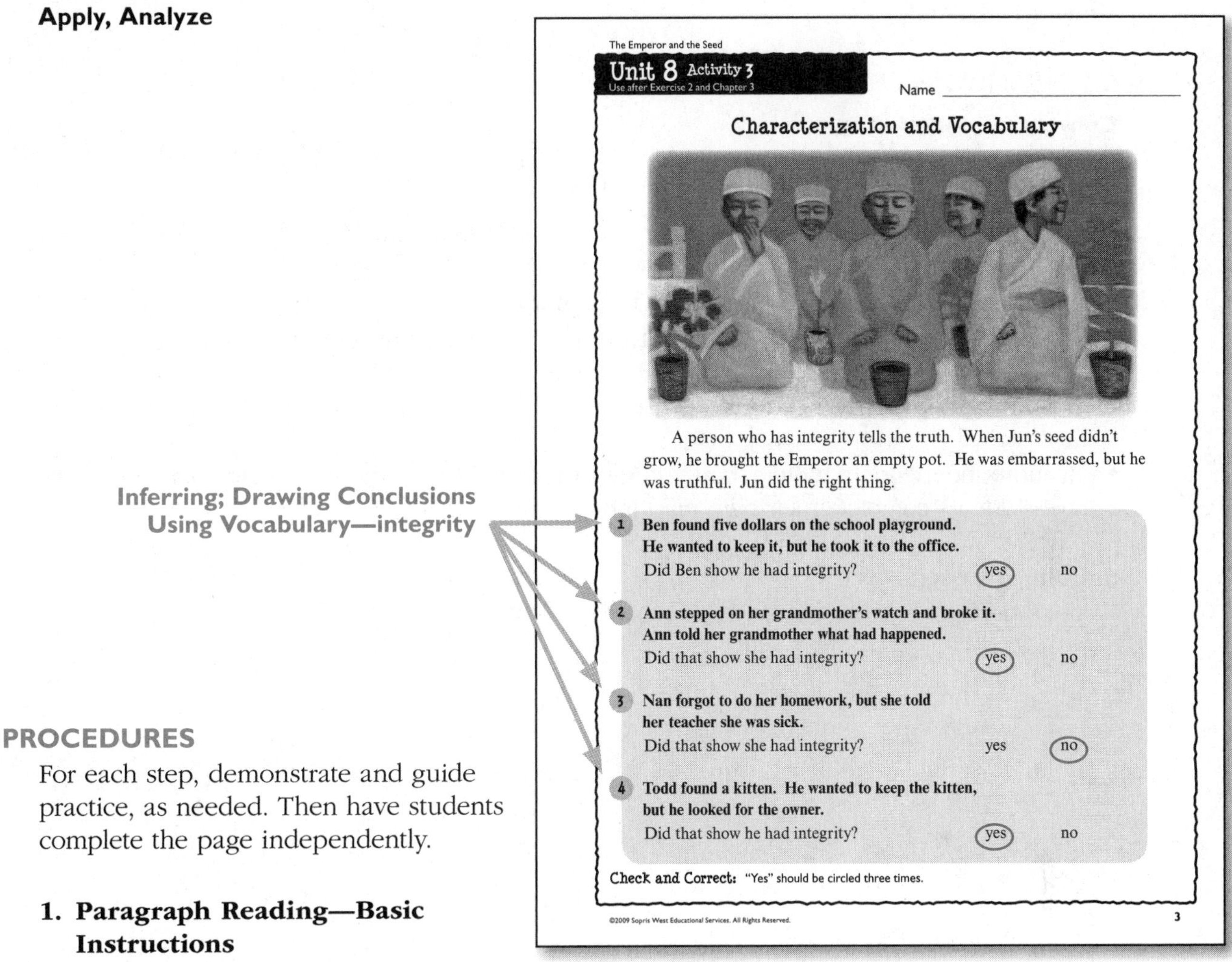

The Emperor and the Seed

Unit 8 Activity 3
Use after Exercise 2 and Chapter 3

Name ______________________

Characterization and Vocabulary

A person who has integrity tells the truth. When Jun's seed didn't grow, he brought the Emperor an empty pot. He was embarrassed, but he was truthful. Jun did the right thing.

1. **Ben found five dollars on the school playground. He wanted to keep it, but he took it to the office.**
   Did Ben show he had integrity? (yes) no
2. **Ann stepped on her grandmother's watch and broke it. Ann told her grandmother what had happened.**
   Did that show she had integrity? (yes) no
3. **Nan forgot to do her homework, but she told her teacher she was sick.**
   Did that show she had integrity? yes (no)
4. **Todd found a kitten. He wanted to keep the kitten, but he looked for the owner.**
   Did that show he had integrity? (yes) no

Check and Correct: "Yes" should be circled three times.

©2009 Sopris West Educational Services. All Rights Reserved. 3

PROCEDURES

For each step, demonstrate and guide practice, as needed. Then have students complete the page independently.

1. **Paragraph Reading—Basic Instructions**
   Have students read the paragraph that defines the word "integrity."

2. **Characterization: Selection Response—Basic Instructions** (Items 1–4)
   - Tell students that they will read each sentence, then decide whether the sentence describes a person with integrity.
   - Have students read Item 1. Guide students as they think about the answer. Say something like:
     Read Item 1. (Ben found five dollars on the school playground. He wanted to keep it, but he took it to the office. Did Ben show he had integrity?)
     Let's think about it. A person who has integrity is honest. He or she does the right thing. Ben took the five dollars to the office. Did that show integrity? (yes)
     Why? (The money didn't belong to him. The right thing was to take the money to the office so they could find who it belonged to. The honest thing to do was return the money.)
     That's right. Ben's actions showed he was honest and truthful.
     Does that show that Ben has integrity? (yes)
     Yes, so we should circle the word *yes*. This shows that Ben has integrity.
   - Repeat with remaining items, as needed.

STORY MAP

COMPREHENSION PROCESSES

Understand, Apply

WRITING TRAITS

Conventions—Period

PROCEDURES

Use an overhead BLM copy of the story map to demonstrate and guide practice, as needed.

Story Map: Character Web, Sentence Completion—Basic Instructions

- Have students complete each section of the story map: introduction, beginning, middle, and end. Remind students to put a period at the end of a sentence.
- For some groups, provide students with time to complete each section before you move to the next.
- For more independent writers, orally guide students through the story map, as needed, then have students complete their own map independently.

Self-monitoring

Have students check and correct their work.

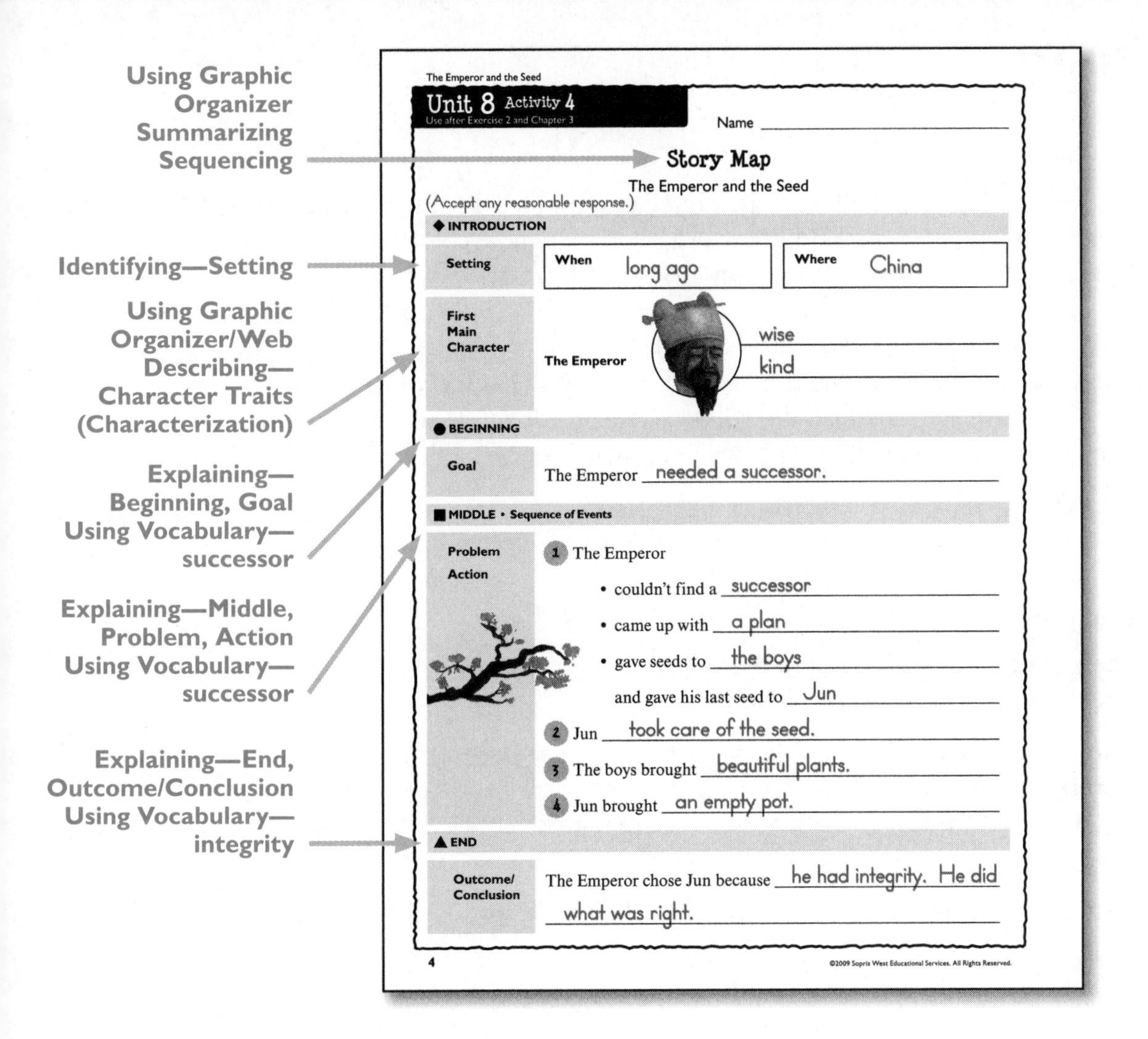

The Emperor and the Seed

Unit 8 Activity 4
Use after Exercise 2 and Chapter 3

Name ______

Story Map

The Emperor and the Seed

(Accept any reasonable response.)

◆ **INTRODUCTION**

Setting — **When** long ago — **Where** China

First Main Character — **The Emperor**: wise, kind

● **BEGINNING**

Goal — The Emperor needed a successor.

■ **MIDDLE** • Sequence of Events

Problem Action

1. The Emperor
   - couldn't find a successor
   - came up with a plan
   - gave seeds to the boys

   and gave his last seed to Jun
2. Jun took care of the seed.
3. The boys brought beautiful plants.
4. Jun brought an empty pot.

▲ **END**

Outcome/Conclusion — The Emperor chose Jun because he had integrity. He did what was right.

4

©2009 Sopris West Educational Services. All Rights Reserved.

❶ SOUND REVIEW

Use selected Sound Cards from Units 1–8.

❷ SOUND PRACTICE

- For each task, have students spell and say the focus sound in the gray bar. Next, have students read each underlined sound, the word, then the whole column.
- Repeat with each column, building accuracy first, then fluency.

❸ ACCURACY AND FLUENCY BUILDING

- For each task, have students say any underlined part, then read the word.
- Set a pace. Then have students read the whole words in each task and column.
- Provide repeated practice, building accuracy first, then fluency.

B1. Related Words

- Tell students the words in each set are related to each other.
- Have students read each word.

C1. Multisyllabic Words

For each word, have students read the syllables, then the whole word.
Use the words in sentences, as needed.

middle	Maya sits on my right. Ben sits on my left. I am sitting in the . . . *middle.*
minstrels	We all enjoyed the music played by the traveling . . . *minstrels.*
recorder	A musical instrument that is like a flute is called a . . . *recorder.*

D1. Word Endings

Have students read any underlined part, then the whole word.

E1. Tricky Words

- For each Tricky Word, have students use the sounds and word parts they know to silently sound out the word. Use the word in a sentence to help with pronunciation.

talked	My sister was on the phone for hours. She . . . *talked* . . . for hours.
through	The fog was thick, but we could walk right . . . *through* . . . it.
stomachs	We ate a lot at the party. Our . . . *stomachs* . . . were full.

- Have students go back and read the whole words in the column.

❹ WORDS IN CONTEXT

For each word, have students use the sounds and word parts they know to silently sound out the word. Then have students read the sentences. Assist, as needed.

The Emperor and the Seed

Unit 8 Exercise 3

Use before rereading Chapters 1–3

1. SOUND REVIEW Use selected Sound Cards from Units 1–8.

2. SOUND PRACTICE In each column, have students spell and say the sound, then say any underlined sound and the word. Next, have students read the whole column.

kn	ce	ow as in snow	Bossy E
knows	dance	show	poke
knowing	advice	bowls	square
known	Cedric	grow	stare
knew	notice	window	homemade

3. ACCURACY AND FLUENCY BUILDING For each column, have students say any underlined part, then read each word. Next, have students read the whole column.

A1 Mixed Practice	B1 Related Words	C1 Multisyllabic Words	D1 Word Endings	E1 Tricky Words
start	travel	mid•dle	strolled	talked
stew	traveler	min•strels	sensed	through
drift	traveling	re•cord•er	strummed	stomachs
gentle	village	middle	setting	
meals	villagers	minstrels	whispering	
spell	villages	recorder		

4. WORDS IN CONTEXT For each word, have students use the sounds and word parts they know to figure out the word. Then have them read the sentences.

A	mu•sic	I love to listen to music.
B	soup	Mom makes delicious chicken soup.
C	scarce	During the winter, deer cannot find food. Food is scarce.
D	ap•pre•ci•ate	I am thankful for your help. I appreciate your help.

LEARNING FROM MISTAKES (Reminder)

Mistakes are an important part of learning!

- If you hear a mistake, say something like: Oops, that was hard, but we can get it!
- Demonstrate or guide students on the correct skill or strategy (sound, sounding out, reading a word by parts . . .).
- Have the group practice the skill.
- Make sure the individual who made the mistake has an opportunity to demonstrate that he or she worked hard and got it.
- Give descriptive feedback. [Shoshannah], you worked hard and now you can read the Tricky Word *through*.

THE EMPEROR AND THE SEED INSTRUCTIONS

Students reread the entire story with the teacher and complete an oral Character Comparison Matrix.

COMPREHENSION PROCESSES

Remember, Understand, Analyze, Evaluate

PROCEDURES

1. Chapter 1, Partner Reading or Whisper Reading: Repeated Reading

Summarizing

Have students finger track and partner or whisper read the selection and summarize Chapter 1.

2. Chapter 2, Group Reading: Repeated Reading

- Ask questions and discuss the story as indicated by the gray text.
- Mix group and individual turns, independent of your voice. Have students work toward a group accuracy goal of 0–4 errors. Quietly keep track of errors made by all students in the group.
- After reading the story, practice any difficult words. Reread the story if students have not reached the accuracy goal.

> **CORRECTING DECODING ERRORS**
> During story reading, gently correct any error, then have students reread the sentence.

3. Chapter 3, Short Passage Practice: Developing Prosody, Repeated Reading

- Demonstrate expressive, fluent reading of the first two paragraphs.
- Guide practice with your voice.
- Provide individual turns while others track with their fingers and whisper read.
- Repeat with one or two more paragraphs.
- Have students read the remainder of the chapter and complete the oral story retell and character comparison.

4. Comprehension and Skill Work

Tell students they will do Comprehension and Skill Activities 5a and 5b. Guide practice, as needed. For teacher directions, see pages 50 and 51.

5. Homework, Teacher's Choice: Repeated Reading

WITH THE TEACHER

Chapter 1

The Emperor

In ancient times, there was a wise and beloved emperor. He ruled the land with fairness and kindness. With no children of his own, the Emperor needed to choose his successor.

Word spread rapidly across the empire. Wealthy parents brought their children from all over the land. Each mother was certain her child would be chosen.

What was the Empero[r] ... a successor?

10

ON YOUR OWN

Chapter 2

The Seed

Again, the children were summoned to the palace. A long line of boys formed around the palace wall. One by one, the boys entered the palace. One by one, the boys in their fine silks were given a small seed. Each boy was told to plant the seed and bring it back in the spring. Each boy placed his seed in a small silk bag.

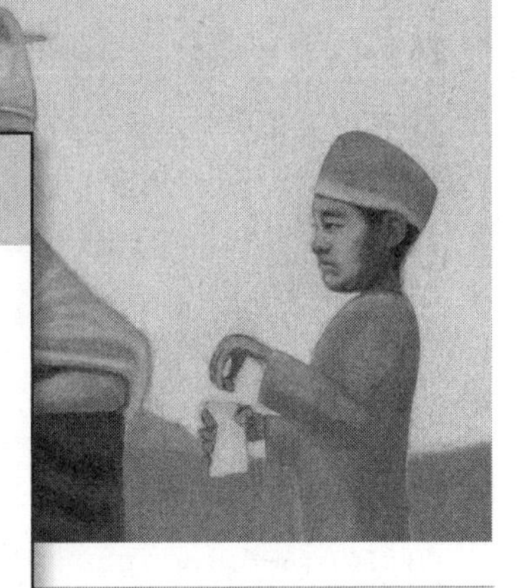

...peror wants the boys to do? How do you think ...peror?

13

WITH THE TEACHER

Chapter 3

The Successor

Across the land, children planted their seeds in beautiful bowls. Jun planted his seed in an ordinary clay pot. Then the boy took care of the seed—just as his grandfather had taught him.

He gave the seed fish food. He watered, and he weeded, and he left the pot in the warm spring sun. To his great surprise, nothing happened.

Jun asked his grandfather for advice. His grandfather said, "Be patient. Some plants need time."

When spring came, children across the land could be seen with big plants in their pots. Each child bragged, "Mine is best. The Emperor will choose me."

Jun was embarrassed. Nothing grew in his pot. Still, he watered, and he weeded, and he made sure that sunlight warmed the pot.

Finally, the children were asked to bring their plants to the palace. Jun did not want to go. His grandfather said, "You must go, Jun. When it is your turn, tell the Emperor that you have done your best."

18

★ 6. Introducing the Character Comparison Matrix

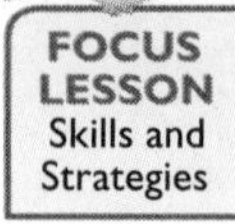

Using Graphic Organizer; Identifying—Main Characters; Explaining—Goals, Problems, Actions, Outcome/Conclusion; Comparing/Contrasting; Drawing Conclusions; Responding

- Tell students that they are going compare the two main characters. Say something like:

  We're going to use a story map to retell the story and compare the main characters. Touch the words "Main Characters." Who are the main characters in this story? (the Emperor, Jun)

- Have students identify and compare the main characters' goals, problems, and actions.
  Think aloud with students.

  The Emperor and Jun both had goals. Read the Emperor's goal. (to find a successor)
  What was Jun's goal? (to plant the seed and grow a plant . . .)
  Did they have the same goals? (no)
  Jun and the Emperor had very different goals!

  Read the Emperor's problem and actions.
  (First, the Emperor couldn't find a successor. Next . . .)

  Now we need to figure out Jun's goal, his problem, and his actions.
  What was Jun's goal? (His goal was to grow a beautiful plant.)
  Did Jun want to become the successor? (no)
  It seems like he just wanted to do his best.
  The Emperor's goal was to find a successor. Jun's goal was simply to grow a plant.

  What was his problem? (He cared for the seed, but it didn't grow.)
  What did Jun do? (He took his empty pot to the Emperor.)

- Have students identify and compare outcomes for the Emperor and Jun.
  Read the Emperor's conclusion.
  (The Emperor chose Jun to be his successor because Jun had integrity.)
  What was the conclusion for Jun?
  (He became the successor because he did not try to trick the Emperor. He was honest.)

- Do you think the Emperor and Jun were the same or different? Why?
  (I think they were the same because they . . .)
  (I think they were different because . . .)

- Discuss the lesson: Be honest and you will be rewarded.
  If you got to choose the Emperor's successor, who would you pick? Why?

★ = New in this unit

WITH THE TEACHER

Story Retell

The Emperor and the Seed

Character Comparison

Setting (When/Where): In ancient times, in China		
Main Characters		
Goals	**Emperor's Goal:** To find a successor	**Jun's Goal:**
Problem	**Emperor's Problem:** First, the Emperor couldn't find a successor.	**Jun's Problem:**
Action	**Emperor's Action:** Next, the Emperor gave seeds to the boys. He gave Jun the last seed. In the spring, the Emperor summoned the boys back.	**Jun's Action:**
Outcome/ Conclusion	The Emperor chose Jun to be his successor because Jun had integrity.	
Lesson	Be honest and you will be rewarded.	

22

WRITTEN RETELL

COMPREHENSION PROCESSES

Remember, Understand, Apply, Evaluate

WRITING TRAITS

Ideas and Content Organization—Sequencing
Conventions—Complete Sentence, Capital, Period
Presentation

Summarizing, Sequencing

Explaining—Setting, Main Characters
Describing—Character Traits (Characterization)

Explaining—Beginning, Goal

Summarizing—Middle, Problem, Action

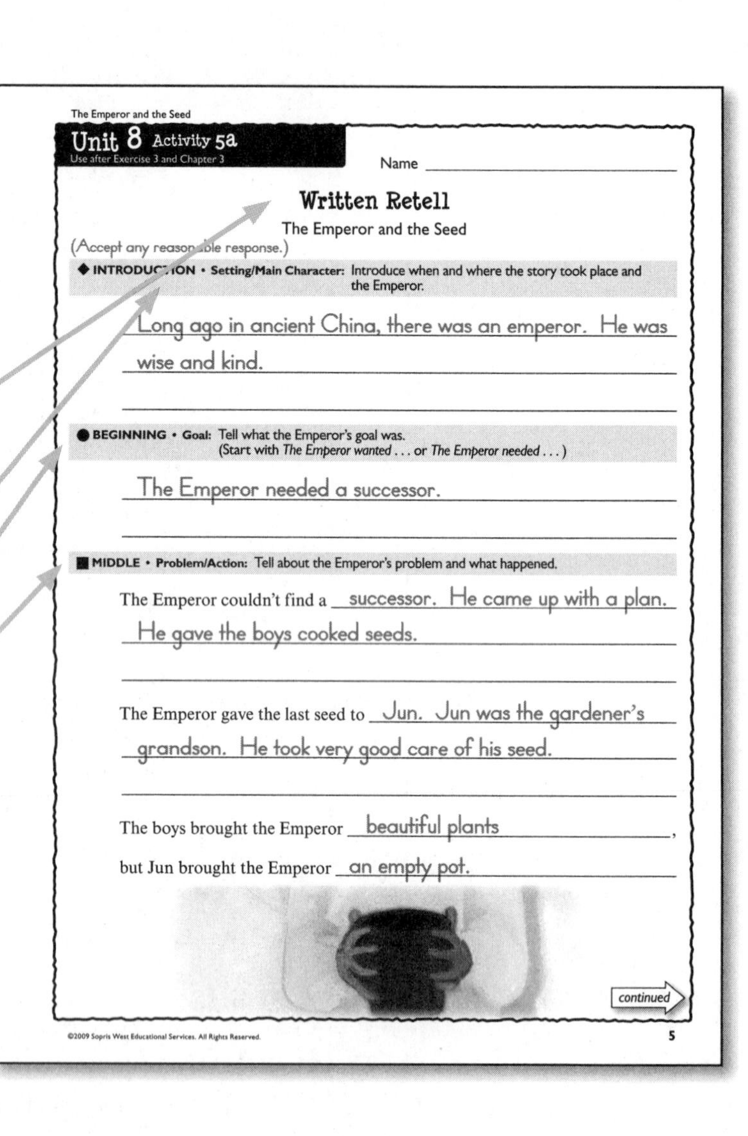

The Emperor and the Seed

Unit 8 Activity 5a
Use after Exercise 3 and Chapter 3

Name ______

Written Retell
The Emperor and the Seed

(Accept any reasonable response.)

◆ INTRODUCTION • Setting/Main Character: Introduce when and where the story took place and the Emperor.

Long ago in ancient China, there was an emperor. He was wise and kind.

● BEGINNING • Goal: Tell what the Emperor's goal was. (Start with *The Emperor wanted . . .* or *The Emperor needed . . .*)

The Emperor needed a successor.

■ MIDDLE • Problem/Action: Tell about the Emperor's problem and what happened.

The Emperor couldn't find a successor. He came up with a plan. He gave the boys cooked seeds.

The Emperor gave the last seed to Jun. Jun was the gardener's grandson. He took very good care of his seed.

The boys brought the Emperor beautiful plants,

but Jun brought the Emperor an empty pot.

continued

©2009 Sopris West Educational Services. All Rights Reserved.

5

PROCEDURES

Use an overhead BLM copy of the story map to demonstrate and guide how to create a written retell.

Written Retell—Basic Instructions

- Guide students, only as needed, as they construct an introductory paragraph using the information from their story map. Before they start, you may wish to brainstorm phrases that describe the main character.
- Repeat for the beginning and middle of the story, using information from the story map. Remind students to start each sentence with a capital and end with a period.

Note: This story has two main characters—the Emperor and Jun. Because Jun is introduced later, the sequential retell begins as the story does by introducing only the Emperor.

WRITTEN RETELL (*continued*)

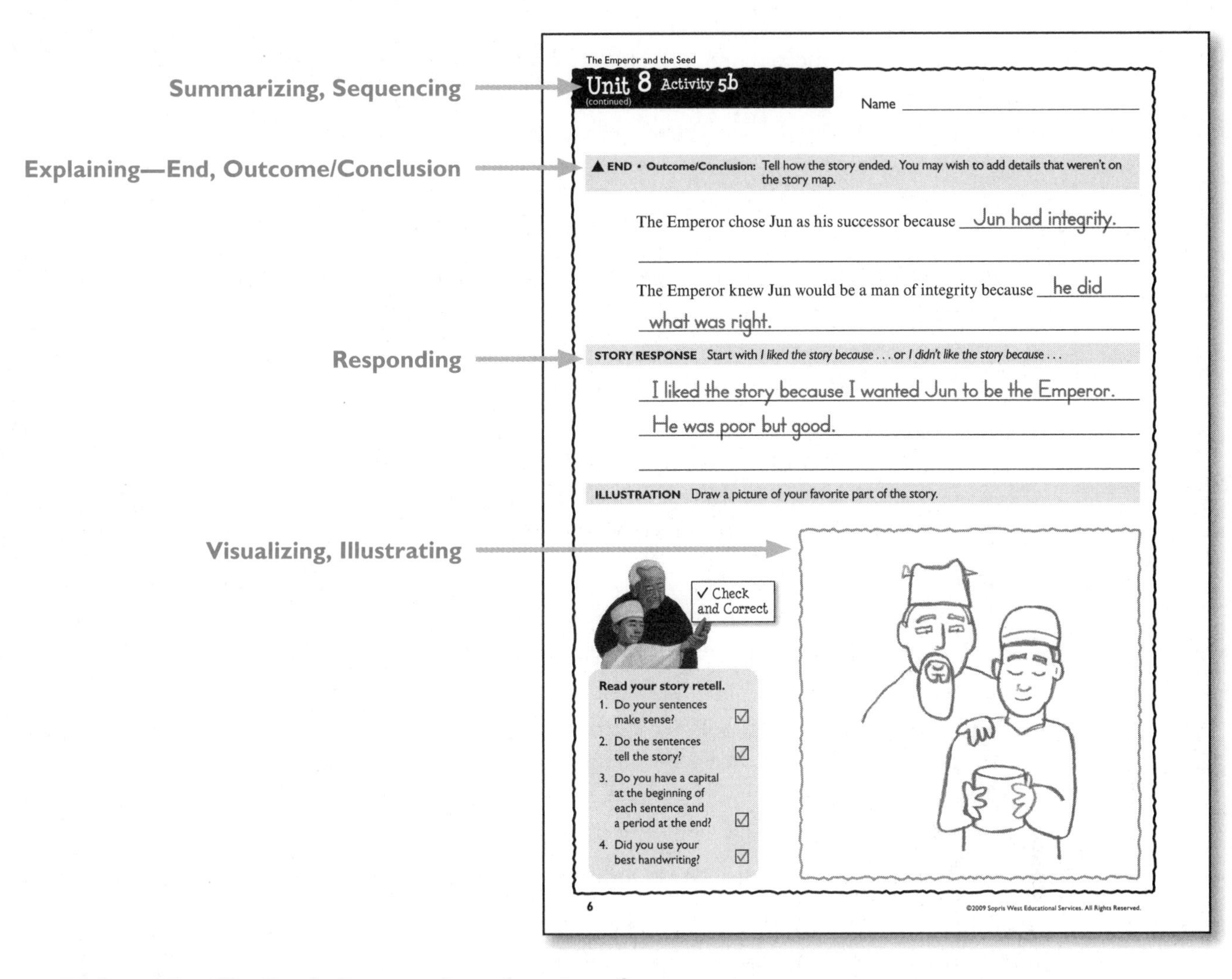

The Emperor and the Seed

Unit 8 Activity 5b (continued)

Name ____________

▲ END • Outcome/Conclusion: Tell how the story ended. You may wish to add details that weren't on the story map.

The Emperor chose Jun as his successor because Jun had integrity.

The Emperor knew Jun would be a man of integrity because he did what was right.

STORY RESPONSE Start with *I liked the story because . . .* or *I didn't like the story because . . .*

I liked the story because I wanted Jun to be the Emperor. He was poor but good.

ILLUSTRATION Draw a picture of your favorite part of the story.

Read your story retell.

1. Do your sentences make sense? ☑
2. Do the sentences tell the story? ☑
3. Do you have a capital at the beginning of each sentence and a period at the end? ☑
4. Did you use your best handwriting? ☑

6

©2009 Sopris West Educational Services. All Rights Reserved.

Written Retell—Basic Instructions (*continued*)

- Guide students as they complete an ending paragraph based on information in the story map.
- Have students write a complete sentence explaining why they liked or did not like the story.
- Have students check and correct their work, then illustrate their favorite part of the story.

❶ SOUND REVIEW

Use selected Sound Cards from Units 1–8.

PACING

Exercise 4a should take about 10 minutes, allowing about 10 minutes for the Maze Reading Focus Lesson.

★❷ NEW SOUND INTRODUCTION

- Have students look at the picture. Tell students p-h says /fff/ as in phone.

  Look at the picture. Say "p-h says /fff/ as in phone." (p-h says /fff/ as in phone)

  Listen to the p-h words in the sentence. "Phillip's new photo is right next to the phone."

  Read the sentence. (Phillip's new photo is right next to the phone.)

  Which three words have the /fff/ sound? (Phillip's, photo, phone)

- For Row B, have students read the underlined sound, then the word.
- After reading the row, have students go back and read the whole words.

❸ ACCURACY AND FLUENCY BUILDING

E1. Tricky Words

- For each Tricky Word, have students use the sounds and word parts they know to silently sound out the word. Use the word in a sentence to help with pronunciation.
- If the word is unfamiliar, tell students the word. Then have students say, spell, and say it.

merry

Look at the first word. The e-r is tricky. It says *air.* Say the word parts with me. mer-ry

Spell *merry.* (m-e-r-r-y) Jodie was full of joy. He was . . . *merry.* Read the word. (merry)

earned When you get money for working, the money is . . . *earned.*
England English people are from . . . *England.*
stomachs The children ate peaches and filled their . . . *stomachs.*
soup For lunch, I like to eat a sandwich and . . . *soup.*

E2. Story Words

For each word, tell students the underlined sound and have them read the word.

curious My brother always asks lots of questions because he's . . . *curious.*
delicious I think apples are . . . *delicious.*
scrumptious The chocolate cake was . . . *scrumptious.*

❹ WORDS IN CONTEXT

❺ MULTISYLLABIC WORDS

For each word, have students read the syllables, then the whole word.

minstrels Musicians from long ago were called . . . *minstrels.*
recorder A musical instrument that is like a flute is the . . . *recorder.*
contented They were happy. They were . . . *contented.*
instruments Latisha knows how to play eight musical . . . *instruments.*

★ = New in this unit

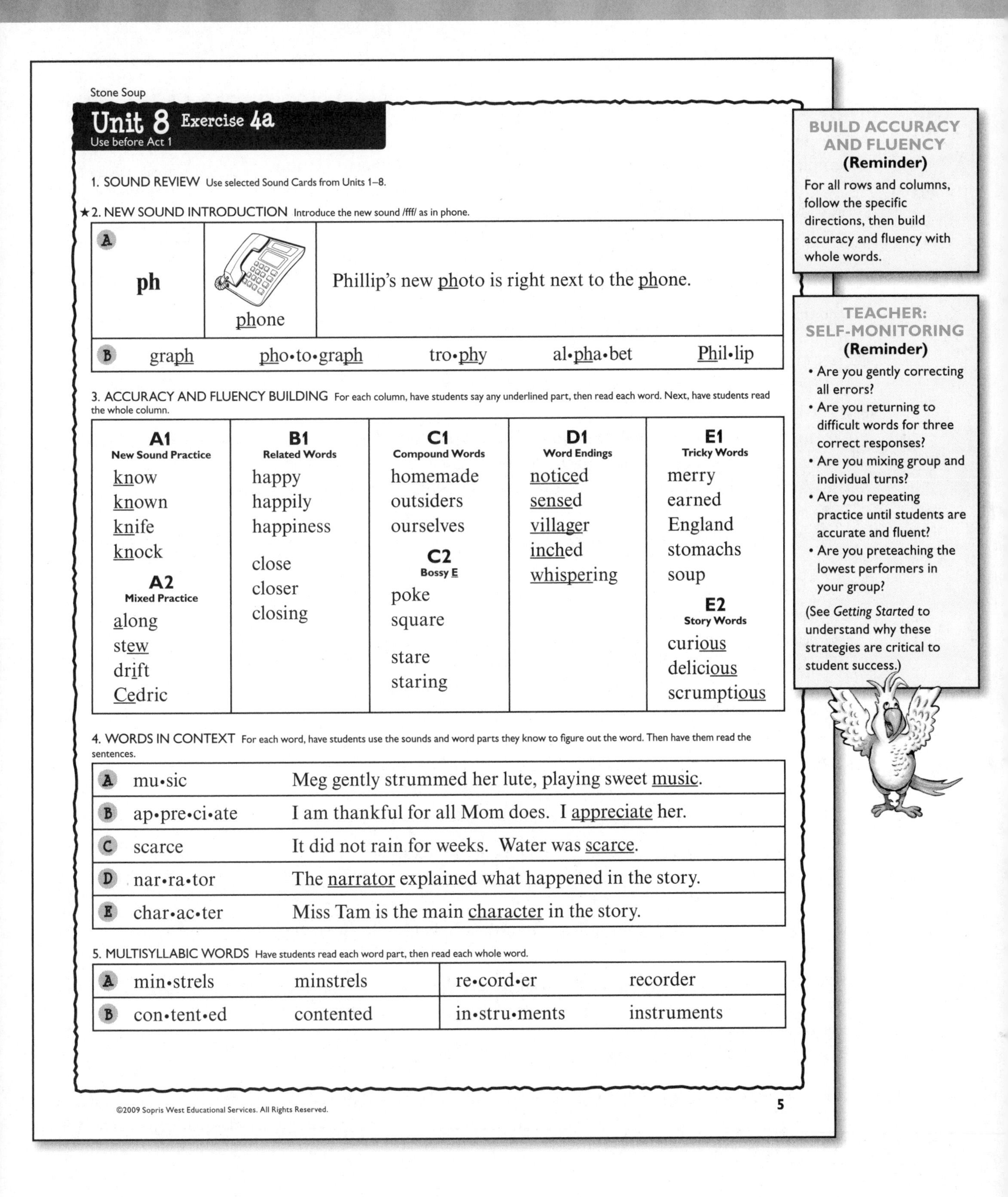

Stone Soup

Unit 8 Exercise 4a

Use before Act 1

1. SOUND REVIEW Use selected Sound Cards from Units 1–8.

★2. NEW SOUND INTRODUCTION Introduce the new sound /fff/ as in phone.

A ph	phone	Phillip's new photo is right next to the phone.

B	graph	pho•to•graph	tro•phy	al•pha•bet	Phil•lip

3. ACCURACY AND FLUENCY BUILDING For each column, have students say any underlined part, then read each word. Next, have students read the whole column.

A1 New Sound Practice	B1 Related Words	C1 Compound Words	D1 Word Endings	E1 Tricky Words
know	happy	homemade	noticed	merry
known	happily	outsiders	sensed	earned
knife	happiness	ourselves	villager	England
knock		**C2** Bossy E	inched	stomachs
A2 Mixed Practice	close	poke	whispering	soup
along	closer	square		**E2** Story Words
stew	closing	stare		curious
drift		staring		delicious
Cedric				scrumptious

4. WORDS IN CONTEXT For each word, have students use the sounds and word parts they know to figure out the word. Then have them read the sentences.

A	mu•sic	Meg gently strummed her lute, playing sweet music.
B	ap•pre•ci•ate	I am thankful for all Mom does. I appreciate her.
C	scarce	It did not rain for weeks. Water was scarce.
D	nar•ra•tor	The narrator explained what happened in the story.
E	char•ac•ter	Miss Tam is the main character in the story.

5. MULTISYLLABIC WORDS Have students read each word part, then read each whole word.

A	min•strels	minstrels	re•cord•er	recorder
B	con•tent•ed	contented	in•stru•ments	instruments

BUILD ACCURACY AND FLUENCY (Reminder)

For all rows and columns, follow the specific directions, then build accuracy and fluency with whole words.

TEACHER: SELF-MONITORING (Reminder)

- Are you gently correcting all errors?
- Are you returning to difficult words for three correct responses?
- Are you mixing group and individual turns?
- Are you repeating practice until students are accurate and fluent?
- Are you preteaching the lowest performers in your group?

(See *Getting Started* to understand why these strategies are critical to student success.)

MAZE READING

PURPOSE

The purpose of this lesson is to provide explicit instruction in how to complete a Maze Reading exercise. This will prepare students for future Comprehension and Skill Work and will also provide students with practice on a maze test-taking format. Students do not write in their books but will watch and respond as you guide them through the lesson.

PREP NOTE

To demonstrate how to complete the Maze Reading activity, use an overhead of page 6 in student *Exercise Book 2*, write on a transparency placed over the page, or use a paper copy.

COMPREHENSION PROCESSES

Understand

PROCEDURES

❶ INTRODUCTION

Explain the purpose of the lesson and how students will learn a strategy for selecting the correct word to complete the sentences in the Maze Reading exercise. Say something like:

Today, we are going to learn how to complete a Maze Reading. A maze is a puzzle.
So this exercise is a puzzle for you. As you read, you'll need to stop and pick the best of three words to complete some of the sentences. If you pick the wrong word, the sentence won't make sense.

❷ MAZE READING

Comprehension Monitoring

- Guide practice in selecting the best word to complete the paragraph.

  Look at the first box. Read the first sentence. (My father is a great cook.)
  The next sentence is tricky. Read the first part and stop at the parentheses.
  (On a cold day, he often . . .)
  The sentence stops, so now we get to choose the next word.
  There are three choices. Let's try reading the whole sentence with the first choice.
  On a cold day, he often . . . *from* . . . a pot of homemade soup.
  Does "*from* a pot of homemade soup" make sense? (no)

  Let's try reading the sentence with just the second word. Read with me.
  On a cold day, he often . . . *makes* . . . a pot of homemade soup.
  Does that sentence make sense? (yes)
  Yes, that sentence does make sense. My father could *make* a pot of soup.
  Let's circle the answer *makes*.

  Let's check the last word to see if it makes sense. Read the sentence with the third word.
  (On a cold day, he often . . . *chops* . . . a pot of homemade soup.)
  Does that sentence make sense? (no)
  No, it doesn't make sense. We don't *chop* a pot of soup. So our answer must be correct.

- Have students read the whole passage to make sure it makes sense.

  Let's read the whole passage to make sure it makes sense. Read the circled word when you get to the parentheses. (My father is a great cook. On a cold day, he often makes a pot of homemade soup.)

Stone Soup

Unit 8 Exercise 4b (Focus Lesson)
Use after Exercise 4a and before Act 1

FOCUS LESSON
Skills and Strategies

Maze Reading

1 Read!

My father is a great cook. On a cold day, he often (from, makes, chops) a pot of homemade soup.

2 Think! Does it make sense?

- On a cold day, he often (**from**, makes, chops) a pot of homemade soup.
- On a cold day, he often (from, **makes**, chops) a pot of homemade soup.
- On a cold day, he often (from, makes, **chops**) a pot of homemade soup.

3 Now you try it!

Sometimes, my father bakes a cake. I think my father is a (for, small, great) cook.

What makes sense?

STOP
Don't write in your Exercise Book.

6 Blackline Master

A PLAY

"Stone Soup" was written as a three-act play, complete with narrators, roles, and a chorus. Read the lesson plan options on pages 7–9 to determine the best way to schedule this portion of the unit.

The last day of the unit includes a rereading of the play. What fun to pretend doing a radio play!

- Invite the principal to listen to your "radio" play.
- Tape record the reading.

SET UP, ASSIGNING ROLES

Suggestion: Write each role on a strip of paper. Have students draw their part from a box or hat.

- Each day, assign new roles.
- Regardless of group size, every student in your group should have a role to read.

STORY READING 4 (Day 4)

ACT 1: A Meal for a Song

Parts for Act 1: Ten active parts and the chorus (All)

Narrator 1 (2 paragraphs)
Narrator 2 (2 paragraphs)
Narrator 3 (1 paragraph)
Narrator 4 (1 short passage)
Old Man (1 short passage)
Young Girl (1 short passage)
Old Woman (no active part)
Young Boy (1 short passage)
Cedric, minstrel (3 short passages)
Ann, minstrel (1 short passage)
Phillip, minstrel (2 short passages)
All (4 paragraphs)

- If you have 10 students, assign each student a part. Every student in the group will choral read the All parts.
- If you have fewer than 10 students, double up on short parts. Every student in the group will choral read the All parts.
- If you have more than 10 students, only the extra students will choral read the All parts.

STORY READING 5 (Day 5)

ACT 2: A Pot of Water and Three Small Stones

Parts for Act 2: Ten active parts and the chorus (All)

Narrator 1 (1 short passage)
Narrator 2 (1 paragraph)
Narrator 3 (2 paragraphs)
Narrator 4 (1 paragraph)
Old Man (no active part)
Young Girl (4 short passages)
Old Woman (1 short passage)
Young Boy (1 short passage)
Cedric, minstrel (2 paragraphs, 1 short passage)
Ann, minstrel (4 short passages)
Phillip, minstrel (2 paragraphs, 1 short passage)
All (2 paragraphs)

- If you have 10 students, assign each student a part. Every student in the group will choral read the All parts.
- If you have fewer than 10 students, double up on short parts. Every student in the group will choral read the All parts.
- If you have more than 10 students, only the extra students will choral read the All parts.

STORY READING 6 (Day 6)

ACT 3: A Luscious Pot of Soup

Parts for Act 2: Nine active parts and the chorus (All)

Narrator 1 (1 short passage)
Narrator 2 (1 paragraph)
Narrator 3 (1 paragraph)
Narrator 4 (1 paragraph)
Old Man (1 short passage)
Young Girl (no active part)
Old Woman (no active part)
Young Boy (1 short passage)
Cedric, minstrel (3 short passages)
Ann, minstrel (3 short passages)
Phillip, minstrel (1 paragraph, 3 short passages)
All (3 paragraphs)

- If you have 9 students, assign each student a part. Every student in the group will choral read the All parts.
- If you have fewer than 9 students, double up on short parts. Every student in the group will choral read the All parts.
- If you have more than 9 students, only the extra students will choral read the All parts.

STORY READING 7 (Day 7)

ACTS 1–3

Parts for Acts 1–3: Eleven active parts and the chorus (All)

Narrator 1 (2 paragraphs, 2 short passages)
Narrator 2 (4 paragraphs)
Narrator 3 (4 paragraphs)
Narrator 4 (2 paragraphs, 1 short passage)
Old Man (2 short passages)
Young Girl (5 short passages)
Old Woman (1 short passage)
Young Boy (3 short passages)
Cedric, minstrel (2 paragraphs, 7 short passages)
Ann, minstrel (8 short passages)
Phillip, minstrel (3 paragraphs, 6 short passages)
All (9 paragraphs)

- If you have 11 students, assign each student a part. Every student in the group will choral read the All parts.
- If you have fewer than 11 students, double up on short parts. Every student in the group will choral read the All parts.
- If you have more than 11 students, only the extra students will choral read the All parts.

COMPREHENSION PROCESSES

Remember, Understand, Apply

PROCEDURES

1. Introducing the Story

Identifying—Title, Setting, Genre, Lesson; Viewing; Inferring; Using Vocabulary—integrity

Have students read the title of their new story, "Stone Soup."
Say something like:

Everyone, turn to page 3.
What's the title of this story? (Stone Soup)
Look at the picture on page 23.
Do you think this story takes place in China? (no)
That's right. It doesn't take place in China. How can you tell?
(The picture doesn't look like China.)

This story takes place in England.
Like "The Emperor and the Seed," the story of "Stone Soup" is a folktale that is hundreds of years old. It also has been told from one generation to the next.

Folktales usually have an important lesson for us. "The Emperor and the Seed" and "Stone Soup" are from different parts of the world, but both stories teach important lessons about people.

Who remembers the lesson in "The Emperor and the Seed"?
(It's important to be honest. Leaders should have integrity . . .)
We will learn another important lesson in "Stone Soup."

We will also have fun reading "Stone Soup." It was written as a play. A play is a story that is written and spoken in parts. Just like a story, a play has a setting, characters, and events that take place.

How did the authors write "Stone Soup"?
(They wrote it as a play.)

3

2. **Setting a Purpose**

   To encourage students' interest in the story's lesson, say something like:

   This story is another one of my favorite stories. It has been told for hundreds of years. At the end of the story, I'll be interested to hear why you think this story has lasted so long.

COMPREHENSION PROCESSES

Remember, Understand, Apply, Evaluate

PROCEDURES

Introducing Vocabulary

★ **folktale** ★ **village**
★ **minstrel, contented**
★ **scarce** ★ **appreciate**
★ **curious**

- For each vocabulary word, have students read the word by parts, then read the whole word.
- Read the student-friendly explanations to students as they follow with their fingers. Then have students use the vocabulary word by following the gray text.
- Review and discuss the photos and illustrations.

USING VOCABULARY

WITH THE TEACHER

Acts 1, 2

Vocabulary

★ **folk•tale**

A **folktale** is a story that people tell each other and pass along from one generation to the next.

The "Emperor and the Seed" is a *folktale.* What country is it from?[1]

★ **vil•lage**

A **village** is like a town, but smaller. A village is a place where people live and work.

The people from the small mountain *village* came into town to buy things. What's a very small town called?[2]

★ **min•strel**

A **minstrel** is a person who lived long ago and traveled from place to place singing and playing music.

If you lived in a village long ago, what would you think if *minstrels* came to your town?[3]

con•tent•ed

Contented means happy and satisfied with something.

What does *contented* mean?[4]
Complete this sentence: After eating the luscious soup, the man was . . .[5]
When do you feel contented?[6]

★ = New

24

1. **Understand:** Identifying—Where; Using Vocabulary—folktale (It's from China.)
2. **Remember:** Using Vocabulary—village (A very small town is called a village.)
3. **Evaluate:** Responding; **Understand:** Using Vocabulary—minstrels (I would be happy if minstrels came because I could watch them sing and dance . . .)
4. **Remember:** Defining and Using Vocabulary—contented (Contented means happy and satisfied with something.)
5. **Apply:** Using Vocabulary—contented (contented)
6. **Apply:** Making Connections; Using Vocabulary—contented (I am contented when I have ice cream for dessert. I am contented when I do a good job on my homework . . .)

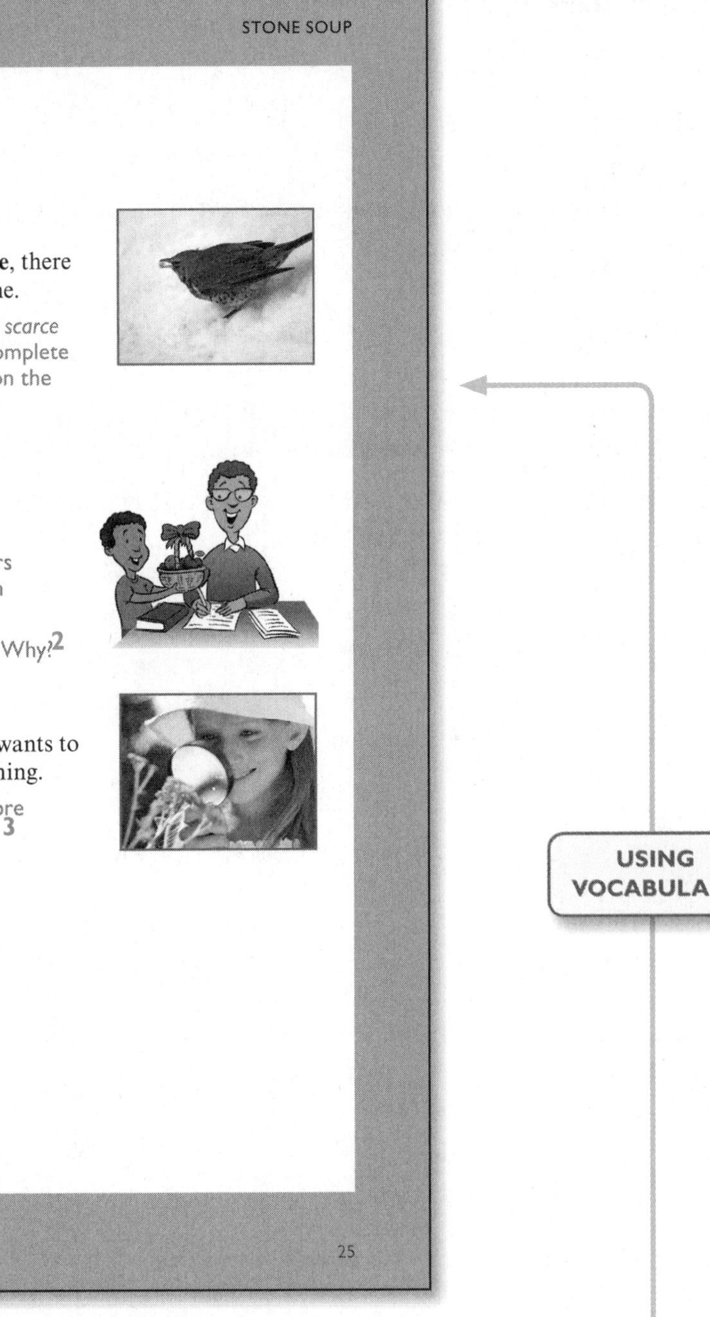

STONE SOUP

★ **scarce**

When something is **scarce**, there is not enough for everyone.

During the winter, food is *scarce* for the forest animals. Complete this sentence: Snow was on the ground so food was . . .[1]

★ **ap•pre•ci•ate**

Appreciate means to be thankful for something.

We *appreciate* the teachers because they help us learn new things.

Who do you appreciate? Why?[2]

★ **cu•ri•ous**

Someone who is **curious** wants to know more about something.

Sandy wanted to learn more about plants. She was . . .[3]

25

USING VOCABULARY

❶ **Understand:** Using Vocabulary—scarce (scarce)

❷ **Apply:** Making Connections; Using Vocabulary—appreciate (I appreciate my mother because she drives me to practice. I appreciate . . .)

❸ **Apply:** Asking Questions (curious)

★ = New in this unit

ACT 1 INSTRUCTIONS

Students will read all three acts of "Stone Soup" with the teacher.

COMPREHENSION PROCESSES

Remember, Understand, Apply

PROCEDURES

1. Introducing Act 1

Identifying—What

- Discuss the parts. Say something like:

  Look at page 26. A play is written in dialogue. *Dialogue* is a snazzy word that means the story is written in the exact words of the characters.

  Take a look at Page 26. Page 26 shows a list of the parts in the play.
  Let's read the parts. Narrator 1 . . .
  What does a narrator do? (A narrator tells the story.)
  We'll read each act more than once, so everyone will get many turns to read.

- Assign parts and introduce the format of the text. Say something like:

  Narrator 1, 2, 3, and 4, All, and the names of the people tell who will read. If it says Narrator 1, who will read?
  If it says Cedric, who will read? If it says All, who will read?

  When it's your turn to read, don't read the name of the character or the name of the part.
  Everyone, turn to page 27. Look at the first part, All. Will you read the word *All*? (no)
  What will you start with? (A merry band of minstrels . . .)

2. First Reading

- Ask questions and discuss the play as indicated by the gray text.
- Have students read their parts.
  Quietly keep track of errors made by all students in the group.
- After reading the story, practice any difficult words and reread, as needed.

3. Second Reading, Short Passage Practice: Developing Prosody

- Demonstrate expressive, fluent reading of the first part.
- Guide practice with your voice.
- Provide individual turns while others track with their fingers and whisper read.
- Repeat with each part, as appropriate.

4. Partner or Whisper Reading: Repeated Reading

Before beginning independent work, have students finger track and partner or whisper read.

5. Comprehension and Skill Work

Tell students they will do Comprehension and Skill Activities 6 and 7 after they read Act 1. Guide practice, as needed. For teacher directions, see pages 69 and 70.

6. Homework 3: Repeated Reading

Act 1

A Meal for a Song

Setting:

A village in England long ago

Characters:

Narrator 1	Young Boy
Narrator 2	Cedric
Narrator 3	Ann
Narrator 4	Phillip
Old Man	All
Young Girl	

All: A merry band of minstrels strolled along a forest path. They talked happily and played sweet music. Ann played her recorder, Cedric strummed his lute, and Phillip told stories through songs.

Narrator 1: The minstrels were contented with what little they had. They earned their meals by singing. People often gave them bowls of homemade stew or freshly baked muffins.

Look at the picture. How did the *minstrels* get their food?[1] Why were they *contented*?[2]

FOCUS ON PROSODY

Encourage students to read with expression. Compliment students on their efforts. Say something like:
[Ann], I liked the way you read "bowls of homemade stew or freshly baked muffins." You made those foods sound so good I could smell the muffins baking.

COMPREHENDING AS YOU GO

❶ **Remember:** Identifying—How; Using Vocabulary—minstrel (The minstrels earned their meals by singing.)

❷ **Understand:** Explaining; Using Vocabulary—contented (The minstrels were contented because they were happy with what they had.)

Narrator 2: As they walked out of the forest, the minstrels noticed a small village. They hoped to find something to eat and a place to sleep.

Narrator 3: The village was poor. Life had been hard for many years. Food was scarce, and the people did not trust outsiders. There was little happiness.

Narrator 4: When the villagers saw the minstrels coming, they closed their windows tight.

All: The children hid. The minstrels sensed eyes staring at them through the cracks around the doors. They could hear whispering.

Describe life in the *village*.[1] Why did the villagers hide from the minstrels?[2]

28

COMPREHENDING AS YOU GO

❶ **Understand:** Describing; Using Vocabulary—village (Life was hard in the village. The people were poor and unhappy.)

❷ **Apply:** Explaining; Using Vocabulary—minstrel (The villagers hid from the minstrels because they didn't trust outsiders.)

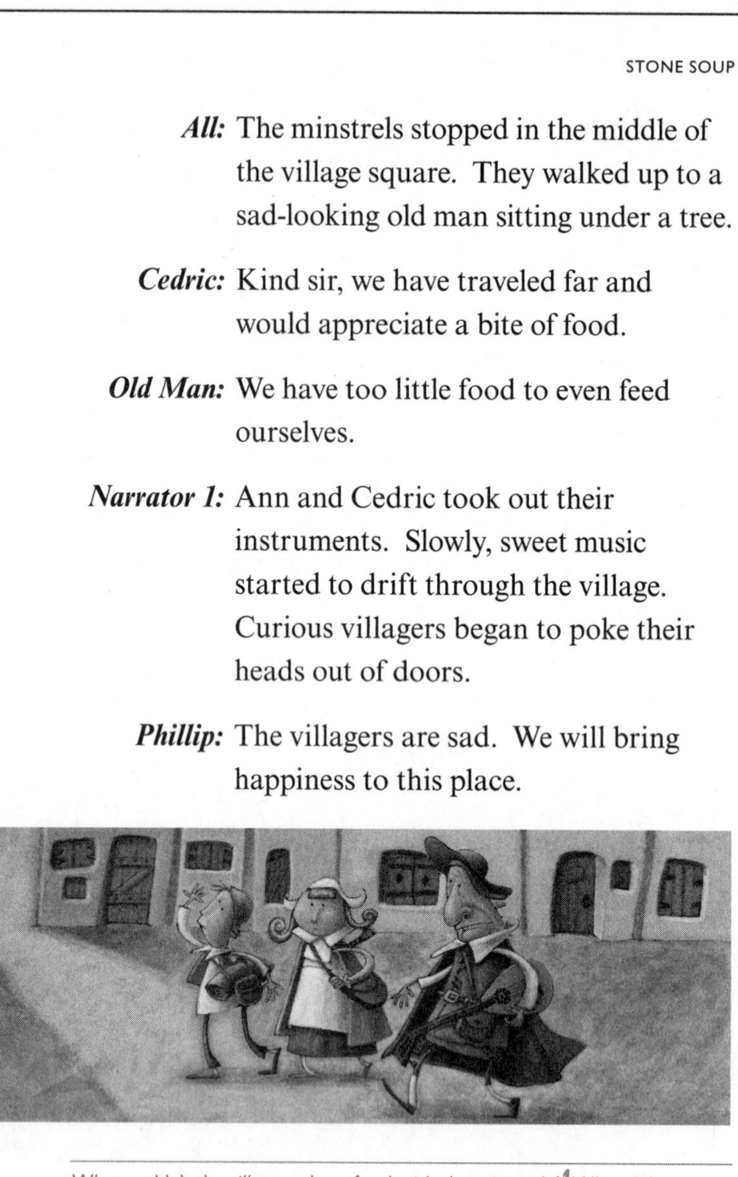

STONE SOUP

All: The minstrels stopped in the middle of the village square. They walked up to a sad-looking old man sitting under a tree.

Cedric: Kind sir, we have traveled far and would appreciate a bite of food.

Old Man: We have too little food to even feed ourselves.

Narrator 1: Ann and Cedric took out their instruments. Slowly, sweet music started to drift through the village. Curious villagers began to poke their heads out of doors.

Phillip: The villagers are sad. We will bring happiness to this place.

Why wouldn't the villagers share food with the minstrels?1 What did the minstrels want to bring to the villagers?2 How could they make the villagers happy?3

29

COMPREHENDING AS YOU GO

1. **Apply:** Inferring, Explaining (The villagers wouldn't share their food because they didn't have enough for themselves.)
2. **Understand:** Explaining—Goal; Using Vocabulary—minstrel, village (The minstrels wanted to bring happiness to the village.)
3. **Apply:** Inferring, Explaining (The minstrels could make the villagers happy by playing music for them . . .)

Narrator 2: Children inched their way closer and closer. A few people gathered and began to hum along with the minstrels.

Ann: The villagers are hungry. Let's bring full stomachs to this village.

Phillip: Cedric, I think it is time for us to make some of your scrumptious stone soup.

Young Girl: Scrumptious. What's that?

Cedric: Scrumptious means delicious. We're going to make a delicious stone soup.

Young Boy: Stone soup. What's that?

Cedric: Ah, stone soup is wonderful for hungry minstrels and their friends.

All: The minstrels had quite a job to do. The village was poor, and the people seemed to have no food. Still, the minstrels were set on making a scrumptious meal for themselves and the villagers.

Reread Narrator 2's part at the top of the page. What do you think is happening to a few of the villagers?1

COMPREHENDING AS YOU GO

1 **Apply:** Inferring; **Understand:** Using Vocabulary—curious, minstrel (Some people are curious about the minstrels. Some people are not hiding from them . . .)

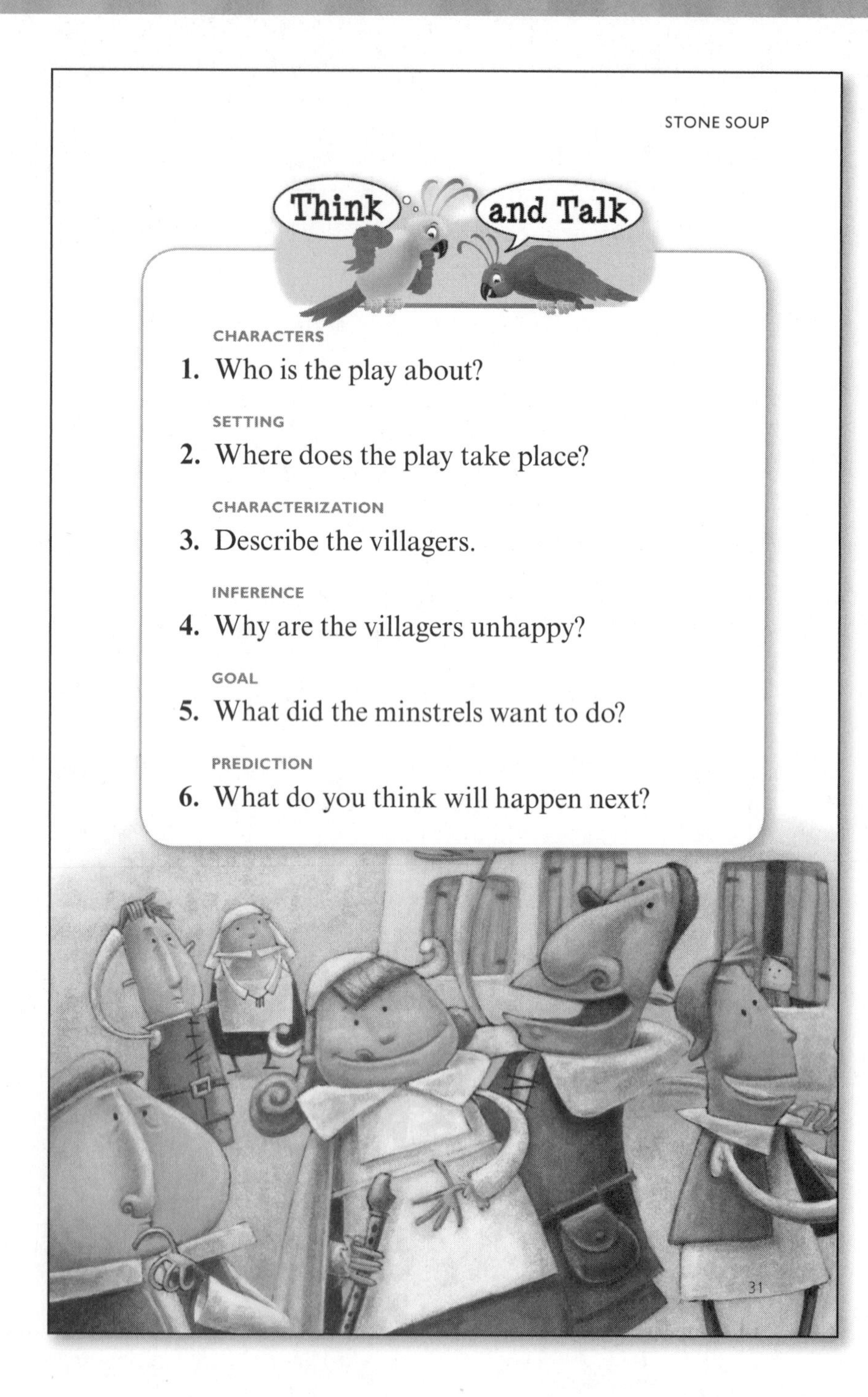

1. **Remember:** Identifying—Main Characters (The play is about three minstrels and the villagers.)
2. **Remember:** Identifying—Setting (It takes place in a small village.)
3. **Understand:** Describing—Character Traits (Characterization) (The villagers were poor and unhappy.)
4. **Apply:** Inferring (The villagers were unhappy because food was scarce.)
5. **Remember:** Identifying—Goal; **Understand:** Explaining (The minstrels wanted to bring happiness to the village.)
6. **Apply:** Predicting (The minstrels will play music for the villagers. The minstrels will make soup for the villagers.)

STORY COMPREHENSION

COMPREHENSION PROCESSES

Remember, Understand, Apply

WRITING TRAITS

Conventions—Complete Sentence, Capital, Period

Identifying—Setting
Using Vocabulary—village

Identifying—Main Characters
Using Vocabulary—minstrel

Identifying—What
Using Vocabulary—minstrel, village

Explaining
Using Vocabulary—minstrel, village

Using Graphic Organizer
Identifying—Goals, Action

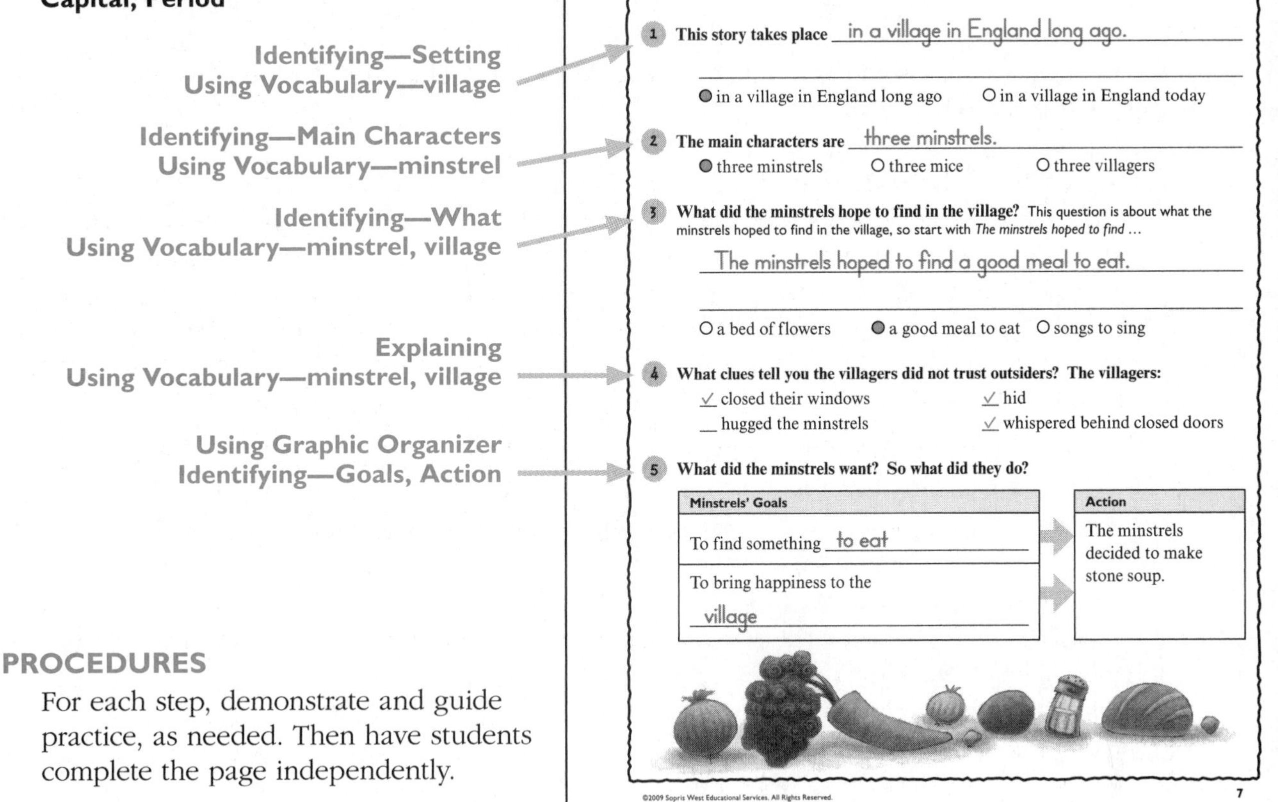

Stone Soup

Unit 8 Activity 6
Use after Exercise 4 and Act 1

Name ______________________

Story Comprehension
A Meal for a Song

1 **This story takes place** in a village in England long ago.

● in a village in England long ago ○ in a village in England today

2 **The main characters are** three minstrels.

● three minstrels ○ three mice ○ three villagers

3 **What did the minstrels hope to find in the village?** This question is about what the minstrels hoped to find in the village, so start with *The minstrels hoped to find ...*

The minstrels hoped to find a good meal to eat.

○ a bed of flowers ● a good meal to eat ○ songs to sing

4 **What clues tell you the villagers did not trust outsiders? The villagers:**

✓ closed their windows
__ hugged the minstrels
✓ hid
✓ whispered behind closed doors

5 **What did the minstrels want? So what did they do?**

Minstrels' Goals	Action
To find something to eat	The minstrels decided to make stone soup.
To bring happiness to the village	

©2009 Sopris West Educational Services. All Rights Reserved.

7

PROCEDURES

For each step, demonstrate and guide practice, as needed. Then have students complete the page independently.

1. **Selection Response—Basic Instructions** (Items 1–4)
   - Have students read each sentence stem or question, then fill in the bubble and/or blank, or check the correct answer.
   - Think aloud with students and discuss the multiple-choice options, as needed.
   - Remind students to start with a capital and end with a period, where needed.

2. **Goal/Action: Sequence Chart—Specific Instructions** (Item 5)
   Have students fill in the blanks to complete the phrases. Explain the relationship between the boxes. Say something like:
   Read item 5. (What did the minstrels want? So what did they do?) The first boxes tell what the minstrels wanted, and the next box tells what the minstrels did to get what they wanted.
   Touch the first box. Read the title. (Minstrels' Goals)
   Read and complete the first stem. What did the minstrels want? (To find something . . . to eat)
   Read and complete the next stem. What else did the minstrels want? (To bring happiness to the . . . village) Yes, the minstrels wanted to find something to eat and to bring happiness to the village. So what did they do? Read the sentence under the Action box. (The minstrels decided to make stone soup.) Yes, the minstrels wanted to find something to eat and to bring happiness to the village, so they decided to make stone soup.

★MAZE READING AND SYNONYMS

COMPREHENSION PROCESSES

Understand, Apply

WRITING TRAITS

Conventions—Period

PROCEDURES

For each step, demonstrate and guide practice, as needed. Then have students complete the page independently.

Maze Reading—Introductory Instructions

- For each box, have students read the sentences and select the word in parentheses that best completes the sentence. Have students circle the word, then reread the paragraph to make sure the whole paragraph makes sense. Say something like:

  We are going to complete a Maze Reading just like we did in our Focus Lesson. Remember, a maze is like a puzzle. You will choose the correct word to complete the sentence. We've already practiced the first box.

  Let's read the second box. Read and stop at the parentheses.
  (Sometimes, my father bakes homemade bread to go with the soup. Then we help him fix a . . .)
  There are three choices. Let's try reading the whole sentence with the first choice.
  (Then we help him fix a . . . *big* . . . green salad.)
  Does that word choice make sense? (yes)
  Yes, it does. Circle *big*, but let's try the next two words to see if either one is better.
  (Then we help him fix a . . . *pink* . . . green salad.)
  Does that make sense? (no)
  Let's try the last word choice. (Then we help him fix a . . . *play* . . . green salad.)
  What do you think? (That's a silly sentence.) So, the first word is best.
  Read the whole box. (Sometimes, my father bakes homemade bread to go with the soup. Then we help him fix a big green salad.)
  Does the whole passage make sense? (yes)

- Repeat with the next box, as needed.

Synonyms: Selection Response—Basic Instructions

- Have students read the directions and main sentence.
- Have students read the numbered sentences, then fill in the bubble and/or blank with the correct answer. Remind students to put a period at the end of the sentence.

★= New in this unit

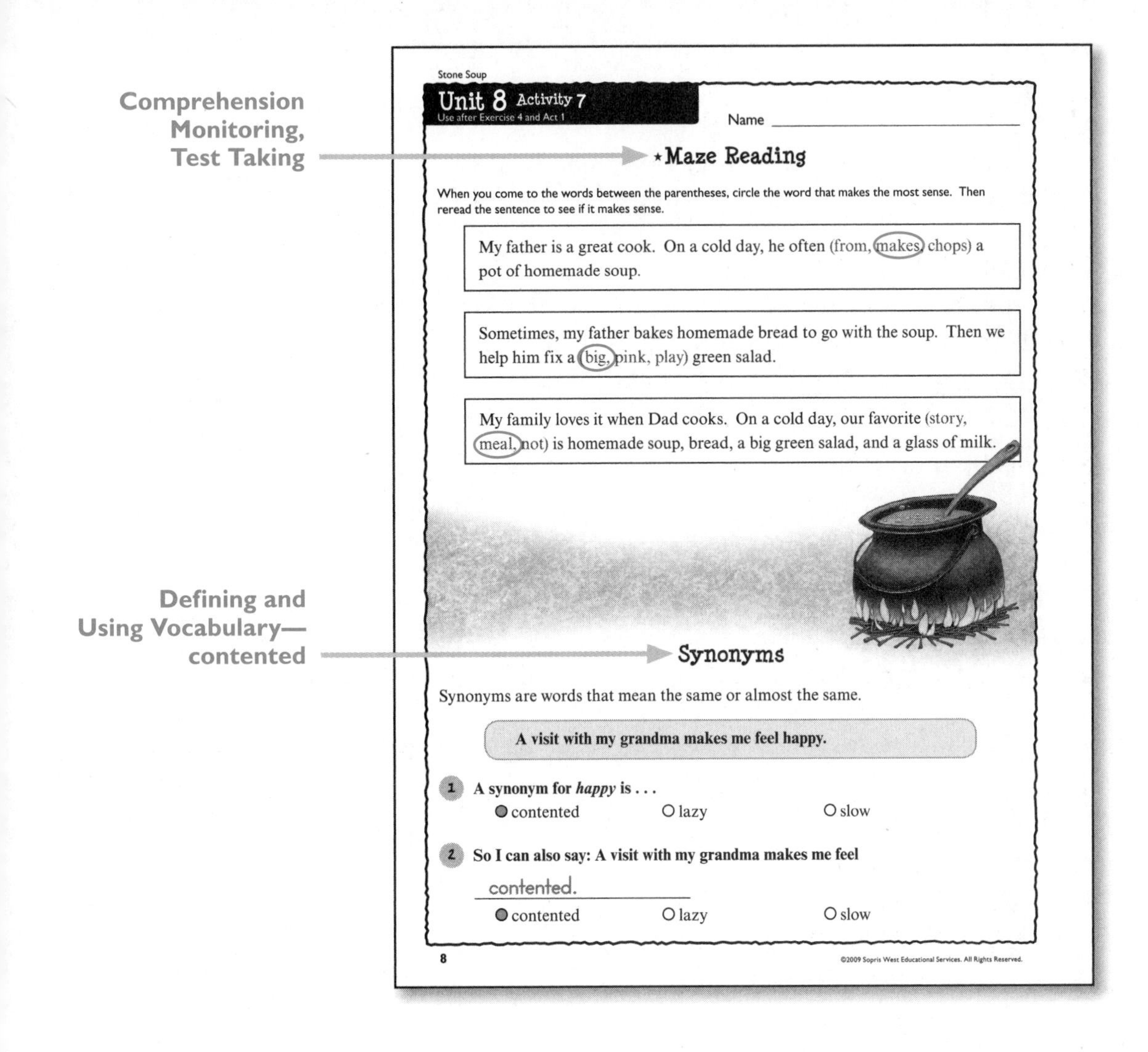

Stone Soup

Unit 8 Activity 7
Use after Exercise 4 and Act 1

Name ____________________

★**Maze Reading**

When you come to the words between the parentheses, circle the word that makes the most sense. Then reread the sentence to see if it makes sense.

My father is a great cook. On a cold day, he often (from, makes, chops) a pot of homemade soup.

Sometimes, my father bakes homemade bread to go with the soup. Then we help him fix a (big, pink, play) green salad.

My family loves it when Dad cooks. On a cold day, our favorite (story, meal, not) is homemade soup, bread, a big green salad, and a glass of milk.

Synonyms

Synonyms are words that mean the same or almost the same.

A visit with my grandma makes me feel happy.

1. **A synonym for *happy* is . . .**
   ● contented ○ lazy ○ slow

2. **So I can also say: A visit with my grandma makes me feel**
   contented.
   ● contented ○ lazy ○ slow

8

❶ SOUND REVIEW

❷ SOUND PRACTICE

For each task, have students spell and say the focus sound in the gray bar. Next, have students read each underlined sound, the word, then the whole column.

❸ ACCURACY AND FLUENCY BUILDING

- For each task, have students say any underlined part, then read the word.
- Set a pace. Then have students read the whole words in each task and column.
- Provide repeated practice, building accuracy first, then fluency.

D1. Story Words

For each word, tell students the underlined sound and have them read the word.

boiling The water got hot and started . . . *boiling.*
luscious The ripe peach was . . . *luscious.*
scrumptious Another word for delicious is . . . *scrumptious.*

E1. Tricky Words

- For each Tricky Word, have students use the sounds and word parts they know to silently sound out the word. Use the word in a sentence to help with pronunciation.
- If the word is unfamiliar, tell students the word. Then have students say, spell, and say it.

enough
Look at the first word. This word is really tricky. The word is *enough.*
Say the word. (enough) Spell it. (e-n-o-u-g-h)
I said I don't want any more. I have had . . . *enough.*
Read the word two times. (enough, enough)

pulled The little boy had a red wagon that he . . . *pulled.*
others Be kind to . . . *others.*
lady Miss Tam is an older . . . *lady.*
onions Tamika loves her hamburgers with . . . *onions.*
certain If you know something for sure, you're . . . *certain.*

❹ MULTISYLLABIC WORDS

For each word, have students read the syllables, then the whole word.

happening What's . . . *happening?*
hungry Jed ate breakfast, so he's not . . . *hungry.*
traveling I love to go . . . *traveling.*
gathering There were many people at the picnic. It was a large . . . *gathering.*

❺ WORDS IN CONTEXT

For each word, have students use the sounds and word parts they know to silently sound out the word. Then have students read the sentence. Assist, as needed.

6 MORPHOGRAPHS AND AFFIXES

- Have students read the underlined part, then the word.
- Review the morphographs *un-* and *-ful* as time allows.
- Repeat practice with whole words, mixing group and individual turns. Build accuracy, then fluency.

Stone Soup

Unit 8 Exercise 5

Use before Act 2

1. SOUND REVIEW Have students review sounds for accuracy, then for fluency.

A	ph	kn	ge	ce	aw
B	or	ay	u	all	ĕ

2. SOUND PRACTICE In each column, have students spell and say the sound, then say any underlined sound and the word. Next, have students read the whole column.

kn	ph	Mixed Practice	
knee	phone	broth	stood
knew	Phillip	Cedric	fire
knock	graph	cracked	stones

3. ACCURACY AND FLUENCY BUILDING For each column, have students say any underlined part, then read each word. Next, have students read the whole column.

A1 Contractions	B1 Word Endings	C1 Rhyming Words	D1 Story Words	E1 Tricky Words
can't	steaming	care	boiling	enough
shouldn't	crackled	share	luscious	pulled
we've	villagers	spare	scrumptious	others
what's	wished	square		lady
	tasted			onions
	salted			certain

4. MULTISYLLABIC WORDS Have students read and finger count each word part, then read each whole word.

A	hap•pen•ing	happening	hun•gry	hungry
B	trav•el•ing	traveling	gath•er•ing	gathering

5. WORDS IN CONTEXT For each word, have students use the sounds and word parts they know to figure out the word. Then have them read the sentence.

A	med•i•cine	I got sick and needed to take medicine to get well.
B	wom•an	A girl grows up to be a woman.

6. MORPHOGRAPHS AND AFFIXES Have students read the underlined word part, then the word.

A	unhappy	determined	wonderful	commotion
B	readable	comfortable	dependable	noticeable

ENCOURAGING DESIRED BEHAVIORS (Reminder)

Make a special effort to notice and congratulate the least mature students whenever they are taking steps toward greater cooperation, responsibility, and independence.

ACT 2 INSTRUCTIONS

Students read Act 2 with the teacher.

COMPREHENSION PROCESSES

Remember, Understand, Apply, Evaluate, Create

PROCEDURES

1. Reviewing Act 1

Identifying—Main Characters, Goals

Have students turn to page 26. Quickly review how the story started, who the main characters are, and what their two goals are—to get a good meal and to help the villagers find happiness.

2. Introducing Act 2

Making Connections, Predicting

- Assign roles. (See page 56 of this teacher's guide.)
- Ask students what they think the minstrels will do next.

3. First Reading

- Ask questions and discuss the play as indicated by the gray text.
- Have students read their parts.
  Quietly keep track of errors made by all students in the group.
- After reading the play, practice any difficult words and reread, as needed.

4. Partner or Whisper Reading: Repeated Reading

Before beginning independent work, have students finger track and partner or whisper read.

5. Comprehension and Skill Work

Tell students they will do Comprehension and Skill Activities 8 and 9 after they read Act 2. Guide practice, as needed. For teacher directions, see pages 82 and 83.

6. Homework 4: Repeated Reading

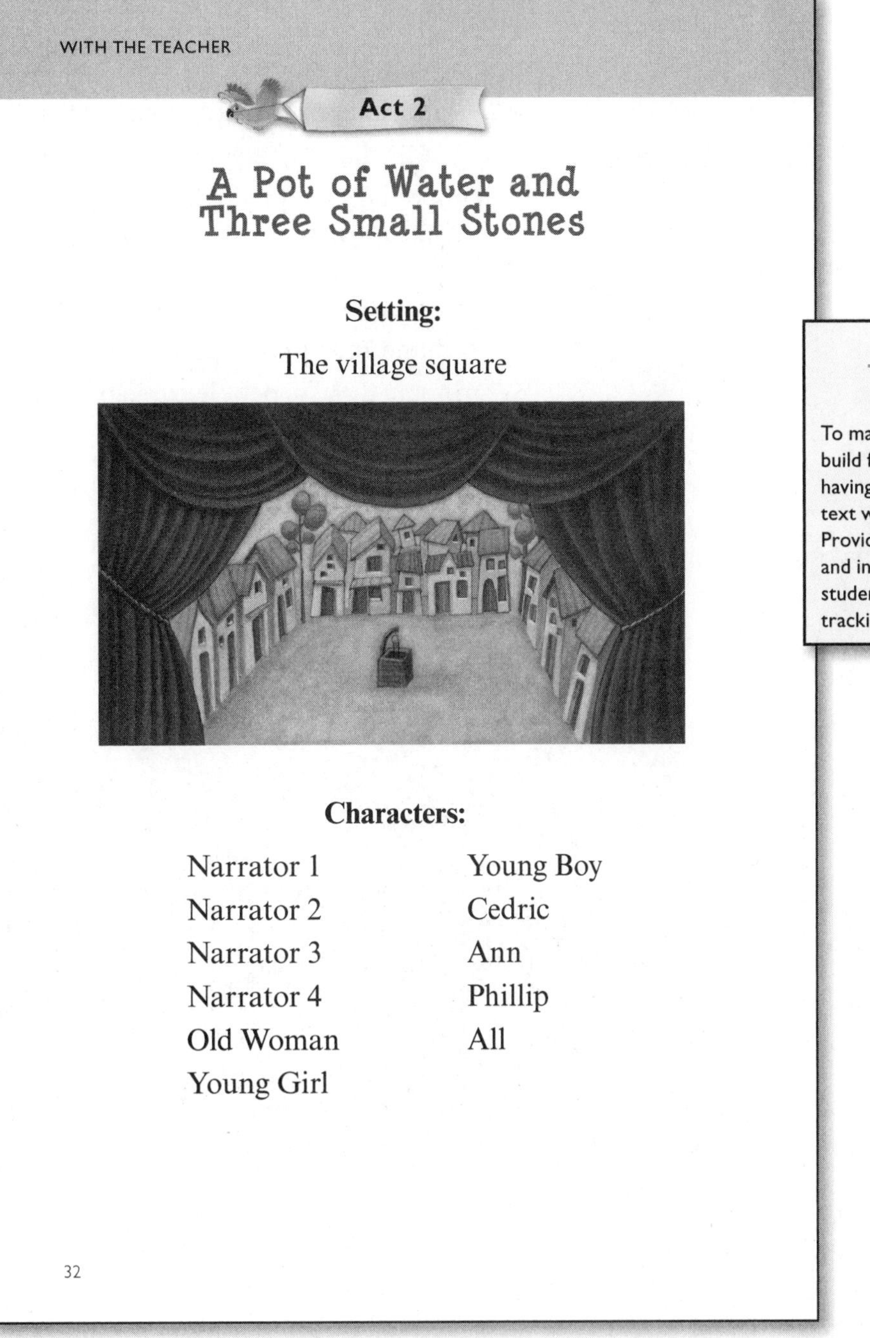

WITH THE TEACHER

Act 2

A Pot of Water and Three Small Stones

Setting:

The village square

Characters:

Narrator 1
Narrator 2
Narrator 3
Narrator 4
Old Woman
Young Girl
Young Boy
Cedric
Ann
Phillip
All

32

FINGER TRACKING (Reminder)

To maintain attention and build fluency, continue having students track text with their fingers. Provide positive feedback and individual turns to students who are finger tracking.

All: Three hungry minstrels had strolled into a village where the people were poor and unhappy. The minstrels were determined to make a scrumptious meal.

Narrator 3: Hearing talk about food, people around the village cracked open their doors. Slowly, people came out of their homes. The minstrels stood in the center of the square.

Describe the villagers.[1] What made them begin to come out of their homes?[2]

COMPREHENDING AS YOU GO

1. **Understand:** Describing (The villagers are poor and unhappy.)
2. **Apply:** Explaining; Using Vocabulary—curious (They heard talk about food. They were curious about the minstrels.)

Ann: We need a fire to make our luscious soup.

Young Girl: Luscious? What's that?

Ann: Luscious means wonderful and delicious. We're going to make a luscious stone soup.

Narrator 4: Ann began gathering sticks, then started a small fire. The young boy and girl helped gather more wood. Others began to help. In no time, a hot fire crackled in the square.

Narrator 1: Phillip pulled out a small pot and three round stones from his pack.

Cedric: We'll need some water.

Young Girl: I'll get some.

Narrator 2: Cedric dropped three stones into the small pot of water. Soon it was steaming.

Do you think the minstrels can make a luscious pot of soup with three stones and water?[1] What would make their soup luscious?[2]

COMPREHENDING AS YOU GO

1. **Evaluate:** Making Judgments (No, stones don't taste good. You can't eat stones . . .)
2. **Create:** Generating Ideas (noodles, meatballs, carrots, garlic, potatoes . . .)

STONE SOUP
35

WITH THE TEACHER

Phillip: It's too bad our pot is so small. If we had a bigger pot, we could make enough soup to share with everyone.

Old Woman: I will let you use my pot.

Phillip: Thank you, kind lady. We will be certain to give you some stone soup.

Narrator 3: Soon the stones were boiling in a bigger pot. More and more villagers gathered to see what the commotion was about. Cedric tasted the soup.

Cedric: Mmm. This broth would be so much better with a bit of salt. But I shouldn't wish for what I can't have.

Young Boy: I can get some salt from my mother.

Phillip: Ah, this stone soup will be very good. But wouldn't some onions make it even more scrumptious?

Who loaned the minstrels a bigger pot?[1] Who will bring salt to the minstrels?[2]

36

COMPREHENDING AS YOU GO

1 **Remember:** Identifying—Who (The old woman loaned the minstrels a bigger pot.)

2 **Remember:** Identifying—Who (The young boy will get some salt from his mother.)

Cedric: Yes, onions would make this the most delicious soup we've ever had. But I should not wish for something I can't have.

Young Girl: My mother says we can spare some onions.

Ann: Oh, kind young girl, we hope you and your mother will have soup with us.

Young Girl: And father too? He is sick in bed.

Ann: Of course! Stone soup is the best medicine for everybody!

All: The village was no longer quiet. More and more people gathered in the square to see what was happening. A pot of salted water sat on a hot fire.

Who will bring onions to the minstrels?1 Why is the village square no longer quiet?2

COMPREHENDING AS YOU GO

1 **Remember:** Identifying—Who (The young girl will bring onions.)

2 **Understand:** Explaining (The village square is not quiet because more and more people are coming to see what is happening.)

1 **Remember:** Identifying—Action (The minstrels are getting the villagers to help make a pot of soup.)

2 **Remember:** Identifying—Goals (The minstrels want to make a pot of soup so they have something to eat, and they also want to bring happiness to the village.)

3 **Understand:** Describing—Character Traits (Characterization) (They are starting to come out of their homes. They are bringing things for the soup. They are starting to talk. The village square is no longer quiet . . .)

PASSAGE READING FLUENCY

FLUENCY

Accuracy, Expression, Rate

PROCEDURES

For each step, demonstrate and guide practice, as needed. Then have students complete the page independently.

Passage Reading—Basic Instructions

- Have students read the practice words first.
- Have students finger track and whisper read the story two times—the first time for accuracy and the second time for expression. Have students cross out a bowl of soup each time they finish.
- Have students do a one-minute Timed Reading and cross out the timer.

Stone Soup

Unit 8 Activity 8
Use after Exercise 5 and Act 2

Name ____________________

Passage Reading Fluency

1. Practice these words:

whined	carrots	peas	corn

2. Read the story 2 times. Cross out a bowl of soup each time you read the story.

A Special Soup Pot

Matt and his sister Jan went for a long walk in the forest. Soon 14
they were very hungry, but they had forgotten to bring lunch. Matt and 27
Jan sat down to rest and saw a large cooking pot under a tree. 41

"Oh, I wish that pot were full of soup," said Jan. Suddenly, a 54
scrumptious smell came from the pot. 60

"Look!" said Matt. "Hot soup to eat." 67

Jan gazed at the soup. "Ick! It has carrots." Zap! The carrots 79
disappeared. 80

"I don't like corn," Matt said. Zap! The corn disappeared. 90

"Why does it have peas?" Jan whined. Zap! The peas disappeared. 101

"Oh, no!" Matt cried. "Now it's just a pot of warm water." 113

Jan shook her head. "We should have appreciated the soup when it 125
was here." 127

The children started home, still very hungry. 134

3. Set a timer and see how far you can read in one minute.
Then cross out the timer.

 9

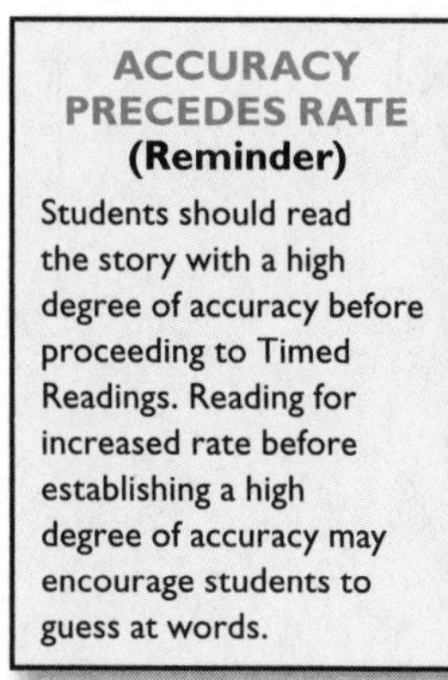
ACCURACY PRECEDES RATE (Reminder)

Students should read the story with a high degree of accuracy before proceeding to Timed Readings. Reading for increased rate before establishing a high degree of accuracy may encourage students to guess at words.

VOCABULARY AND ALPHABETICAL ORDER

COMPREHENSION PROCESSES

Apply

WRITING TRAITS

Conventions—Period

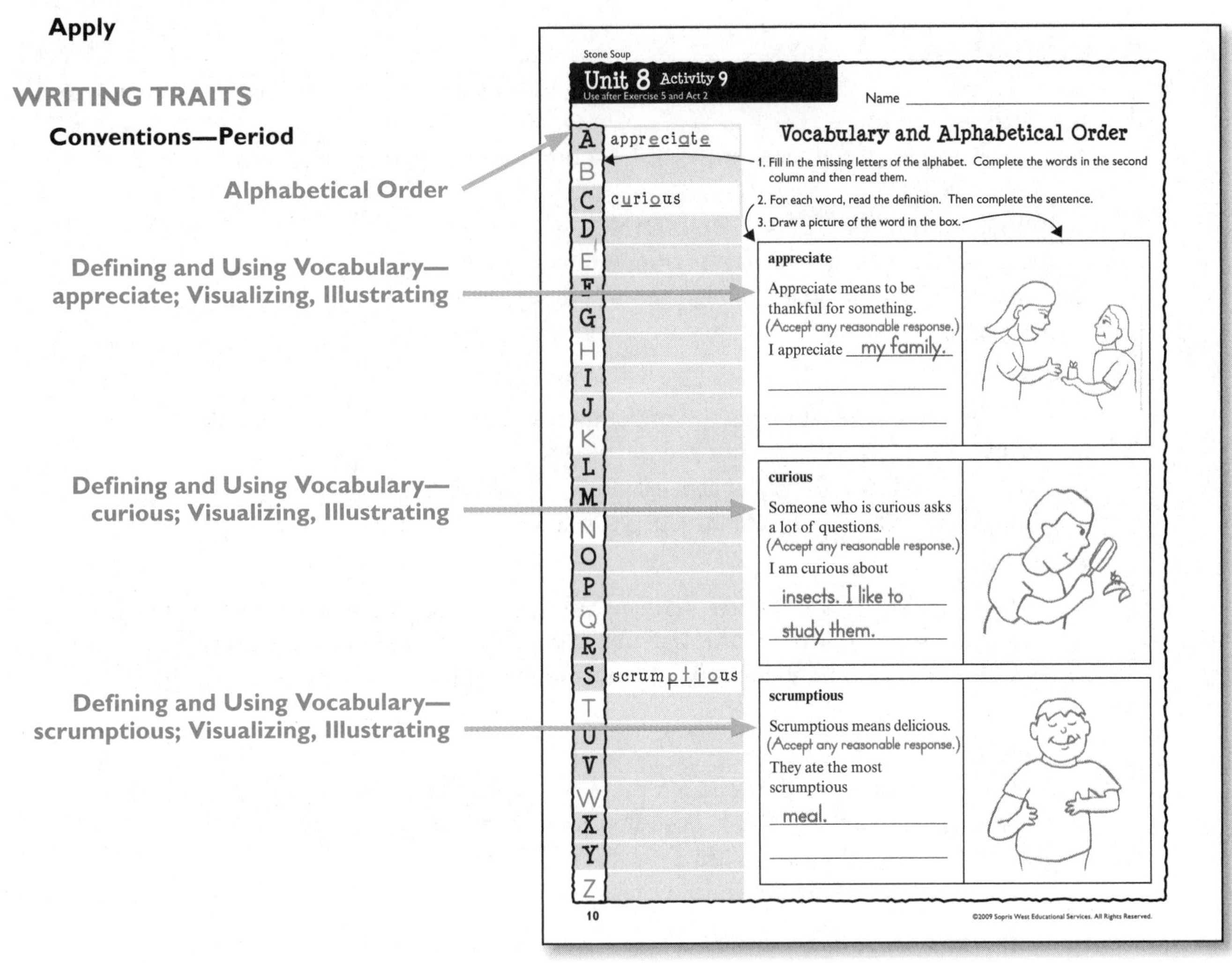

Stone Soup

Unit 8 Activity 9
Use after Exercise 5 and Act 2

Name ______

Vocabulary and Alphabetical Order

1. Fill in the missing letters of the alphabet. Complete the words in the second column and then read them.
2. For each word, read the definition. Then complete the sentence.
3. Draw a picture of the word in the box.

A appreciate
B
C curious
D
E
F
G
H
I
J
K
L
M
N
O
P
Q
R
S scrumptious
T
U
V
W
X
Y
Z

appreciate
Appreciate means to be thankful for something.
(Accept any reasonable response.)
I appreciate my family.

curious
Someone who is curious asks a lot of questions.
(Accept any reasonable response.)
I am curious about insects. I like to study them.

scrumptious
Scrumptious means delicious.
(Accept any reasonable response.)
They ate the most scrumptious meal.

10

©2009 Sopris West Educational Services. All Rights Reserved.

PROCEDURES

For each step, demonstrate and guide practice, as needed. Then have students complete the page independently.

Alphabetical Order—Basic Instructions

- Have students silently read the letters in the alphabet column and fill in the missing letters.
- Have students fill in the blanks for the vocabulary words in the column.

Vocabulary: Sentence Completion, Illustrating—Basic Instructions

- Have students read the vocabulary words and definitions.
- Have students read the sample sentences and fill in the blanks.
- Have students visualize and illustrate each sentence.

Self-monitoring

Have students check and correct their work.

❶ SOUND REVIEW

❷ SHIFTY WORD BLENDING

❸ SOUND PRACTICE

- For each task, have students spell and say the focus sound in the gray bar. For Bossy E, read the header.
- Next, have students read each underlined sound two times, then the word.

❹ ACCURACY AND FLUENCY BUILDING

- For each task, have students say any underlined part, then read the word.
- Set a pace. Then have students read the whole words in each task and column.
- Provide repeated practice, building accuracy first, then fluency.

C1. Story Words

For each word, tell students the underlined sound and have them read the word.

ready It's time to go. Are you . . . *ready?*
joy He felt so much happiness and . . . *joy.*
imagine When you pretend, you . . . *imagine.*

D1, E1. Tricky Words

- For each Tricky Word, have students use the sounds and word parts they know to silently sound out the word. Use the word in a sentence to help with pronunciation.
- If the word is unfamiliar, tell students the word. Then have students say, spell, and say it.

able
Look at the first word. Sound out the word in your head. Thumbs up when you know the word. Use my sentence to help you pronounce the word.
I couldn't do it. I wasn't . . . *able.* Spell it. (a-b-l-e)
Read the word three times. (able, able, able)

poured It rained all day. It . . . *poured.*
watching Andrea felt like someone was . . . *watching* . . . her.
discovered The pirate buried the treasure so it wouldn't be . . . *discovered.*
promised Micah said he would come over Saturday. He . . . *promised.*
brought When Micah came over on Saturday he . . . *brought* . . . his soccer ball.
laughed The joke was funny, so we . . . *laughed.*
eyes Vin's sister has brown hair and blue . . . *eyes.*
young Carlos couldn't drive because he was too . . . *young.*
stomach The roller coaster made Evan feel sick to his . . . *stomach.*

❺ MULTISYLLABIC WORDS

For each word, have students read the syllables, then the whole word.
Use the word in a sentence.

simple Something that isn't complicated is . . . *simple.*
excitement The carnival caused a lot of . . . *excitement.*
contented The purring cat was . . . *contented.*
villagers People who live in a village are called . . . *villagers.*
celery I like peanut butter on . . . *celery.*
potatoes Do you like sour cream on baked . . . *potatoes?*

⑥ MORPHOGRAPHS AND AFFIXES

⑦ GENERALIZATION: READING NEW WORDS IN PARAGRAPHS

Have students read the paragraph silently, then out loud. Tell students to use the sounds and word parts they know to read any difficult words. Repeat practice, as needed.

Stone Soup

Unit 8 Exercise 6
Use before Act 3

1. SOUND REVIEW Use selected Sound Cards from Units 1–8.

2. SHIFTY WORD BLENDING For each word, have students say the underlined part, sound out smoothly, then read the word.

while	whale	stale	stole	stone

3. SOUND PRACTICE In each column, have students spell and say the sound, then say any underlined sound and the word. Next, have students read the whole column.

kn	ph	ew, ue	Bossy E
know	graph	news	cakes
knew	phone	true	times
knee	photo	flew	square

4. ACCURACY AND FLUENCY BUILDING For each column, have students say any underlined part, then read each word. Next, have students read the whole column.

A1 Word Endings	B1 Word Endings	C1 Story Words	D1 Tricky Words	E1 Tricky Words
hugged	hurry	ready	able	brought
chopped	hurried	joy	poured	laughed
sweeten		imagine	watching	eyes
brings	share		discovered	young
spoons	sharing		promised	stomach

5. MULTISYLLABIC WORDS Have students read each word part, then read each whole word.

A	sim•ple	simple	ex•cite•ment	excitement
B	con•tent•ed	contented	vil•lag•ers	villagers
C	cel•er•y	celery	po•ta•toes	potatoes

6. MORPHOGRAPHS AND AFFIXES Have students read each underlined word part, then the word.

departed	finally	comfortable	remained

7. GENERALIZATION Have students read the paragraph silently, then out loud. (New words: Jess, practice, carrots, salad, bread)

When Jess came home from soccer practice, she was hungry. Wonderful smells came from the kitchen. Jess helped her mom set the table. Soon the family was eating a fine meal of steamed carrots, salad, soup, and hot bread.

8

ENTHUSIASM

Make a special effort to acknowledge what students can do.
Say things like:
You can read multisyllabic words without help from adults.
You can figure out words you've never seen before.
You can read and use snazzy words like: *excitement, contented,* and *potatoes*. That is very impressive.

GENERALIZATION (Reminder)

The generalization task provides an opportunity for you to informally assess students' ability to read new words that have not been pretaught.

COMPREHENSION PROCESSES

Understand, Apply

★ imagine, luscious, contented ★ merry, scrumptious ★ wonderful

PROCEDURES

1. Introducing Vocabulary

- For each vocabulary word, have students read the word by parts, then read the whole word.
- Read the student-friendly explanations to students as they follow with their fingers. Then have students use the vocabulary word by following the gray text.
- Review and discuss the photos and illustrations.

USING VOCABULARY

WITH THE TEACHER

Act 3

Vocabulary

★ i•ma•gine

Imagine means to make a picture of something in your mind. You can also imagine how something might smell, taste, and feel.

Imagine flying like a bird. What would it feel like?[1]

*** lus•cious**

Luscious means delicious and mouth-watering. Something that is luscious has a delicious taste or smell.

The ripe peach was . . . *luscious*. Describe a food that you think tastes or smells luscious.[2]

*This word was first defined in the context of the story.

★ = New

39

❶ **Apply:** Making Connections; Using Vocabulary—imagine (It would be exciting. I imagine I could see lots of things. I could have a bird's-eye view of the neighborhood . . .)

❷ **Understand:** Describing; Using Vocabulary—luscious (Watermelon tastes luscious because it's sweet and cool. Cookies smell luscious when they are baking in the oven . . .)

★ = New in this unit

2. Now You Try It!

- Read or paraphrase the directions.
- Then, for each word, have students read the word by parts and then read the whole word.
- Have students explain or define the word in their own words. Say something like:

  Look at the first word. Say the parts, then read the whole word. (scrump•tious, scrumptious)
  Now, let's pretend that we're going to explain or define the word *scrumptious* to a friend. [Reese], what would you say?
  Start with "*Scrumptious* means . . . " (Scrumptious means yummy.)
  That's right. Something yummy is scrumptious. [Ian], how would you explain or define the word *scrumptious?* (Scrumptious means something is so good you want to eat a whole bunch of it.)

- Have students turn to the appropriate page in the glossary and discuss how their definitions are the same as or different from those in the glossary. Your students may like their definitions better.

Note: By defining a word in their own words, students are demonstrating depth of word knowledge. Verbatim responses only demonstrate memorization. Encourage paraphrasing.

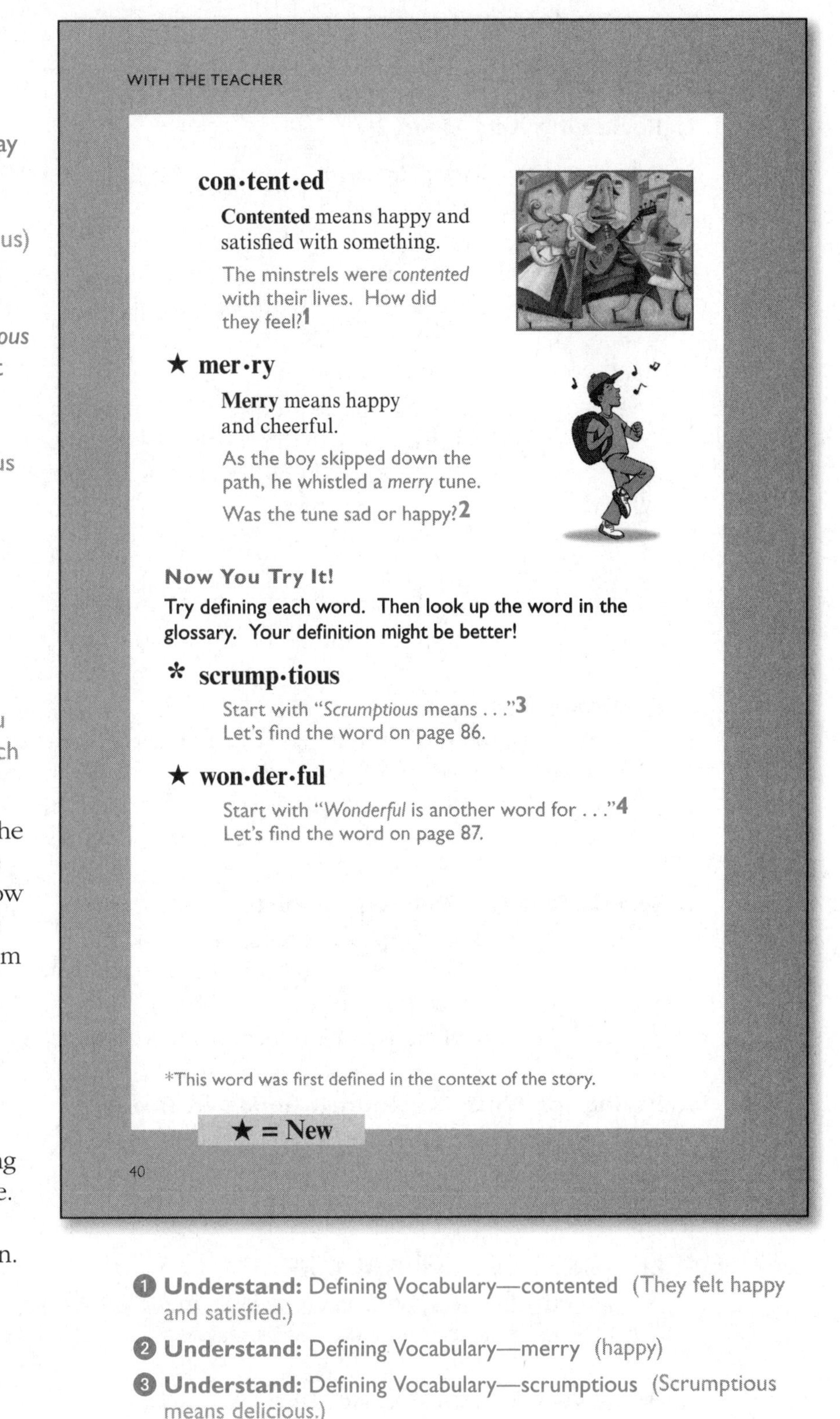

WITH THE TEACHER

con•tent•ed

Contented means happy and satisfied with something.

The minstrels were *contented* with their lives. How did they feel?1

★ **mer•ry**

Merry means happy and cheerful.

As the boy skipped down the path, he whistled a *merry* tune.

Was the tune sad or happy?2

Now You Try It!

Try defining each word. Then look up the word in the glossary. Your definition might be better!

* **scrump•tious**

Start with "*Scrumptious* means . . ."3
Let's find the word on page 86.

★ **won•der•ful**

Start with "*Wonderful* is another word for . . ."4
Let's find the word on page 87.

*This word was first defined in the context of the story.

★ = New

40

❶ **Understand:** Defining Vocabulary—contented (They felt happy and satisfied.)

❷ **Understand:** Defining Vocabulary—merry (happy)

❸ **Understand:** Defining Vocabulary—scrumptious (Scrumptious means delicious.)

❹ **Understand:** Defining Vocabulary—wonderful (Wonderful is another word for excellent, great, or fantastic.)

ACT 3 INSTRUCTIONS

Students read Act 3 with the teacher.

COMPREHENSION PROCESSES

Remember, Understand, Apply, Analyze

PROCEDURES

1. Reviewing Acts 1 and 2

Describing, Predicting, Inferring

Say something like:

What were the villagers like at the beginning of the story? (They were not friendly. They were afraid of others. They were not willing to share. They seemed unhappy.)

At the end of Act 2, people had gathered in the square to see what was happening.

A young boy had brought salt, and a young girl had gone to get onions.

The book says a pot of salted water sat on a hot fire.

Do you think the minstrels will be satisfied with a pot of salted water for their meal? (no)

What do you think is happening to the villagers? (They are curious about the minstrels. They want to have some of the soup.) Are they starting to change? (yes)

What is happening in the story that tells you that the villagers are changing? (They are coming out of their houses. They are sharing things with the minstrels. They aren't so afraid.)

2. Introducing Act 3

Assign parts. (See pages 56 and 57 of this teacher's guide.)

3. First Reading

- Ask questions and discuss the play as indicated by the gray text.
- Have students read their parts.
  Quietly keep track of errors made by all students in the group.
- After reading the play, practice any difficult words and reread, as needed.

4. Second Reading: Rehearsing Parts

- Demonstrate expressive, fluent reading of a part.
  Read at a rate just slightly faster than the students' rate.
- Guide practice with your voice.
- Provide individual turns while others track with their fingers and whisper read.

5. Partner or Whisper Reading: Repeated Reading

Before beginning independent work, have students finger track and partner or whisper read.

6. Comprehension and Skill Work

Tell students they will do Comprehension and Skill Activities 10 and 11 after they read Act 3. Guide practice, as needed. For teacher directions, see pages 96 and 97.

7. Homework 5: Repeated Reading

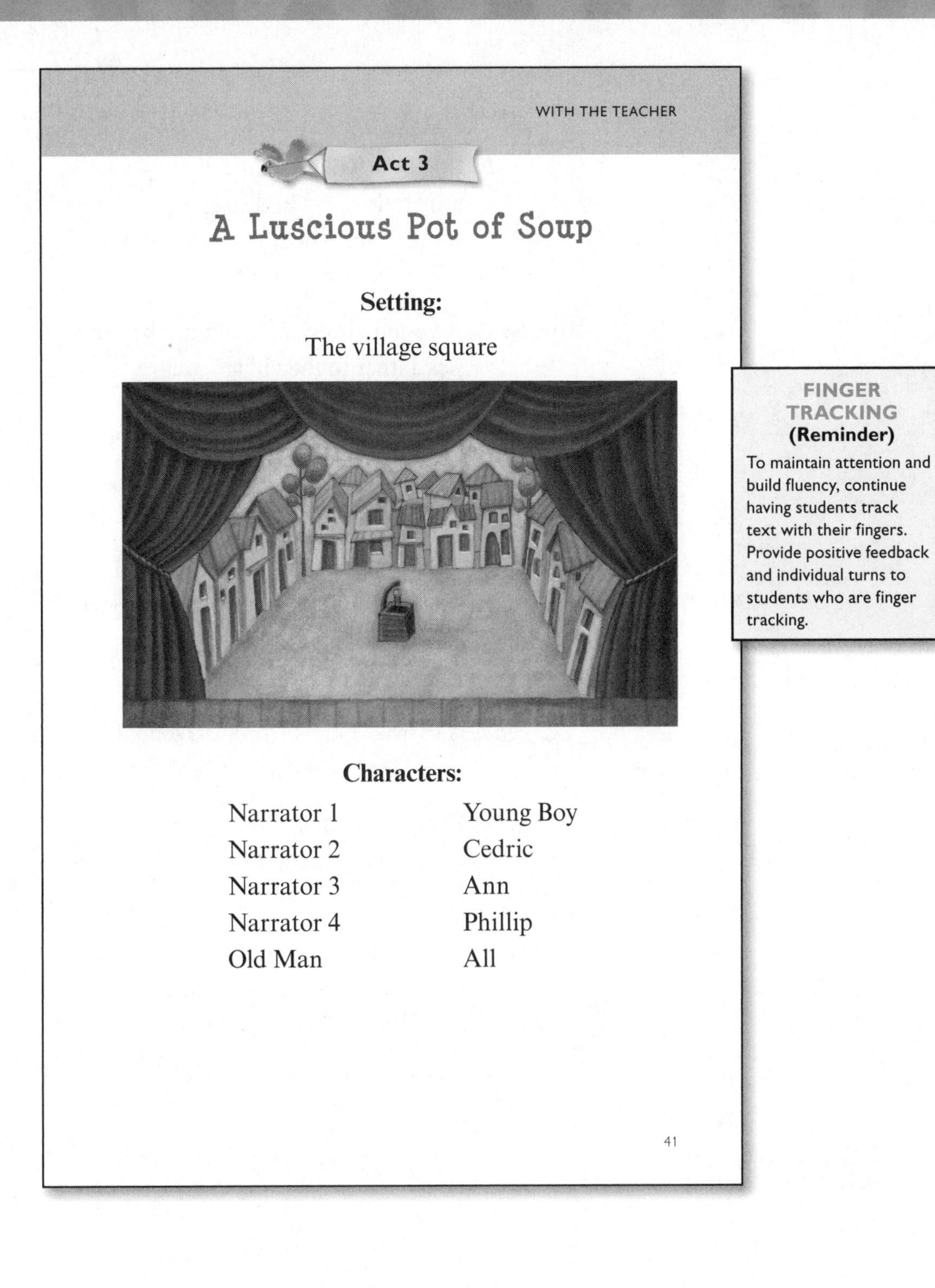

WITH THE TEACHER

Act 3

A Luscious Pot of Soup

Setting:

The village square

Characters:

Narrator 1	Young Boy
Narrator 2	Cedric
Narrator 3	Ann
Narrator 4	Phillip
Old Man	All

41

FINGER TRACKING (Reminder)

To maintain attention and build fluency, continue having students track text with their fingers. Provide positive feedback and individual turns to students who are finger tracking.

All: In a poor village, three hungry minstrels stood in the square making stone soup. The thin soup had only water and a bit of salt.

Narrator 4: A young girl brought her mother and sick father to the village square. Just as she had promised, the girl had a bowl of chopped onions for the soup. She poured the onions into the pot.

Phillip: Hmmm . . . what a wonderful smell. This stone soup will be very good. Imagine if we had a carrot or two to sweeten it up. But I shouldn't wish for what I can't have.

Old Man: A carrot? For a taste of the soup, I may be able to find a carrot to add to the soup.

Cedric: Bring a bunch of carrots and some celery and you shall have a whole bowl of scrumptious soup!

Narrator 1: The old man hurried away and was soon back with carrots and celery.

How are the villagers making the soup better?[1] Some villagers have shared things for the soup. How do you think those villagers feel?[2]

COMPREHENDING AS YOU GO

1. **Apply:** Inferring, Explaining (The villagers are making the soup better by bringing different things to put in it.)
2. **Apply:** Inferring, Making Connections (They feel good because it's nice to share. They are happy because they will get to eat some of the soup . . .)

STONE SOUP
43

WITH THE TEACHER

Phillip: Ah, what a wonderful smell. This will be a very, very good soup.

Cedric: Ann, what was it that made our last stone soup so very, very scrumptious?

Ann: Sweet red potatoes!

Phillip: Ah, sweet red potatoes. That is right. But I shouldn't wish for what I can't have.

Young Boy: My father has a few potatoes that we can put in the soup.

Ann: This stone soup will be just as good as the last pot!

All: One by one, people began to bring something for the soup. For the first time in years, the village square buzzed with excitement. The air was filled with wonderful smells. Finally, the big pot of soup was ready!

The story says, "The village square buzzed with excitement." What do you think that means?1 Why do you think the villagers were excited?2

44

COMPREHENDING AS YOU GO

1 **Apply:** Inferring, Explaining (It means that there was a lot of noise. Everyone was talking about what was going on . . .)

2 **Apply:** Inferring; Explaining; Using Vocabulary—scrumptious (The villagers were excited because they were making something special happen. They were excited because the soup was going to be scrumptious . . .)

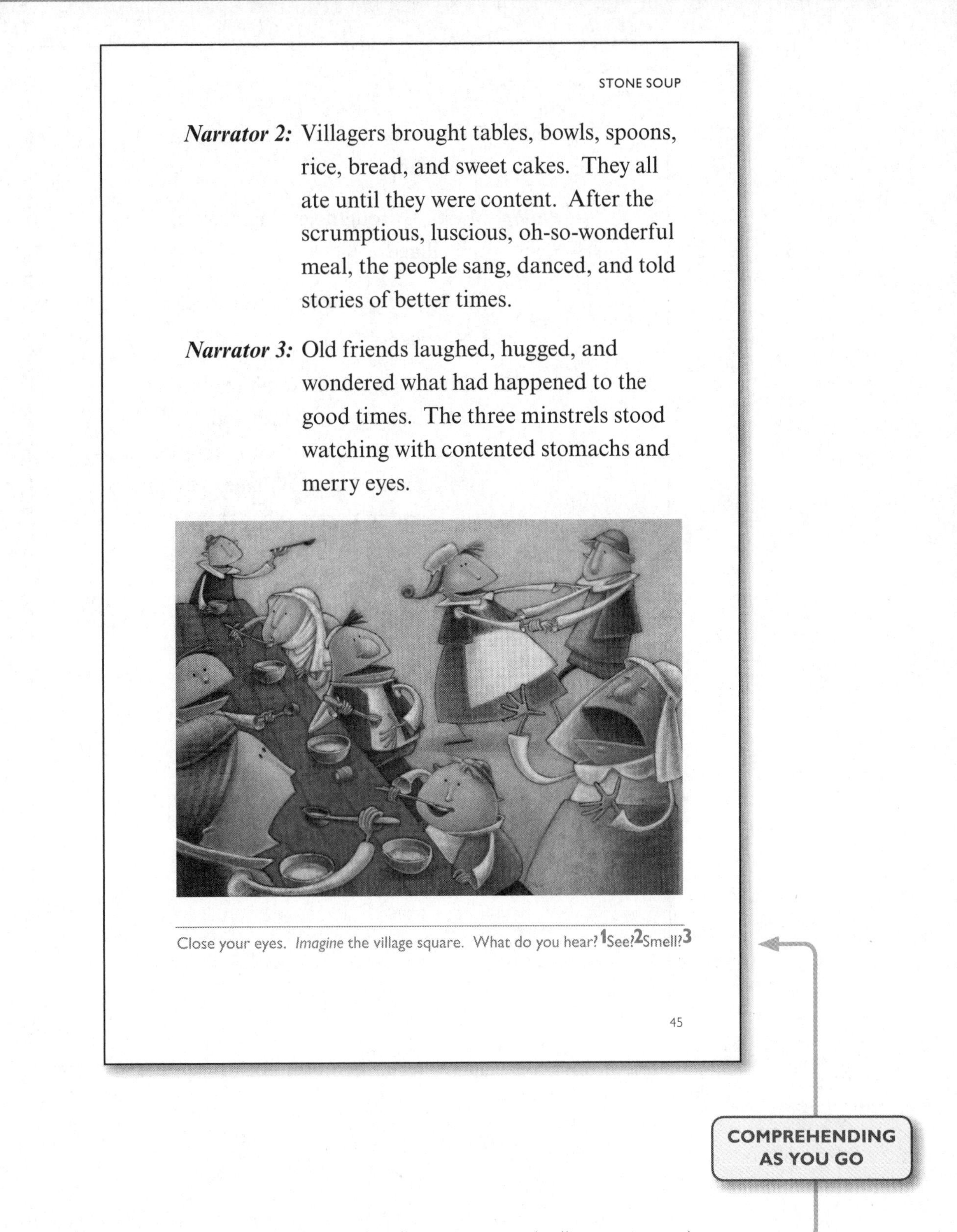

STONE SOUP

Narrator 2: Villagers brought tables, bowls, spoons, rice, bread, and sweet cakes. They all ate until they were content. After the scrumptious, luscious, oh-so-wonderful meal, the people sang, danced, and told stories of better times.

Narrator 3: Old friends laughed, hugged, and wondered what had happened to the good times. The three minstrels stood watching with contented stomachs and merry eyes.

Close your eyes. *Imagine* the village square. What do you hear?[1] See?[2] Smell?[3]

45

COMPREHENDING AS YOU GO

1. **Understand:** Visualizing, Describing (I hear people talking, singing, and telling stories . . .)
2. **Understand:** Visualizing, Describing (I see people eating, hugging, and dancing . . .)
3. **Understand:** Visualizing; Describing; Using Vocabulary—luscious (I smell the luscious soup . . .)

WITH THE TEACHER

Cedric: We have brought togetherness back to the village.

Phillip: We have brought sharing back to the village.

Ann: We have brought happiness back to the village.

All: Sounds of joy drifted in the air as Cedric, Phillip, and Ann departed. Music and song went with them, but it also remained in the village. Happiness was found in the simple making of stone soup.

Why were the villagers contented?[1] What did the minstrels bring to the village?[2] How was happiness found in the making of stone soup?[3]

46

COMPREHENDING AS YOU GO

1. **Apply:** Explaining; Using Vocabulary—contented (The villagers were contented because they ate a scrumptious meal together.)
2. **Understand:** Explaining; Using Vocabulary—village (The minstrels brought togetherness, sharing, and happiness back to the village.)
3. **Analyze:** Drawing Conclusions (People were happy because they shared what they had to make soup. They came out of their houses and spent time together.)

8. Introducing the Story Retell and Story Comparison

FOCUS LESSON
Skills and Strategies

Using Graphic Organizer; Identifying—Title; Explaining—Setting, Goal, Action, Conclusion, Lesson; Comparing/Contrasting

- Tell students they are going to use a graphic organizer to compare "Stone Soup" with "The Emperor and the Seed."
- Have students read the title of each story, then discuss the setting. Say something like:

  The two folktales we read in this unit are alike in many ways. This story comparison will help us see how the stories are the same and how they are different.

  Let's start with the setting. What does the setting tell us? (when and where)

  When and where did "Stone Soup" take place? (in England, long ago)

  Where and when did "The Emperor and the Seed" take place? (in China, long ago; in ancient China)

  How were the settings different? (They took place in different countries.)

  How were the settings the same? (They are both very old stories.)

- Repeat with each story element.

WITH THE TEACHER

Story Comparison

Traditional Tales

Story	Stone Soup	The Emperor and the Seed
Setting: Where and when	**England, long ago**	
Goal	**Minstrels' goal:** To get a good meal **Minstrels' goal for the villagers:**	**Emperor's goal:** **Jun's goal:**
Action	**Minstrels' action:** Made stone soup **Villagers' action:**	**Emperor's action:** **Jun's action:**
Conclusion	The villagers helped make stone soup and discovered happiness.	
Lesson	Sharing and community bring happiness.	

47

MAIN IDEA AND SUPPORTING DETAILS

COMPREHENSION PROCESSES

Remember, Understand, Apply

WRITING TRAITS

Conventions—Complete Sentence, Beginning Capital, Period

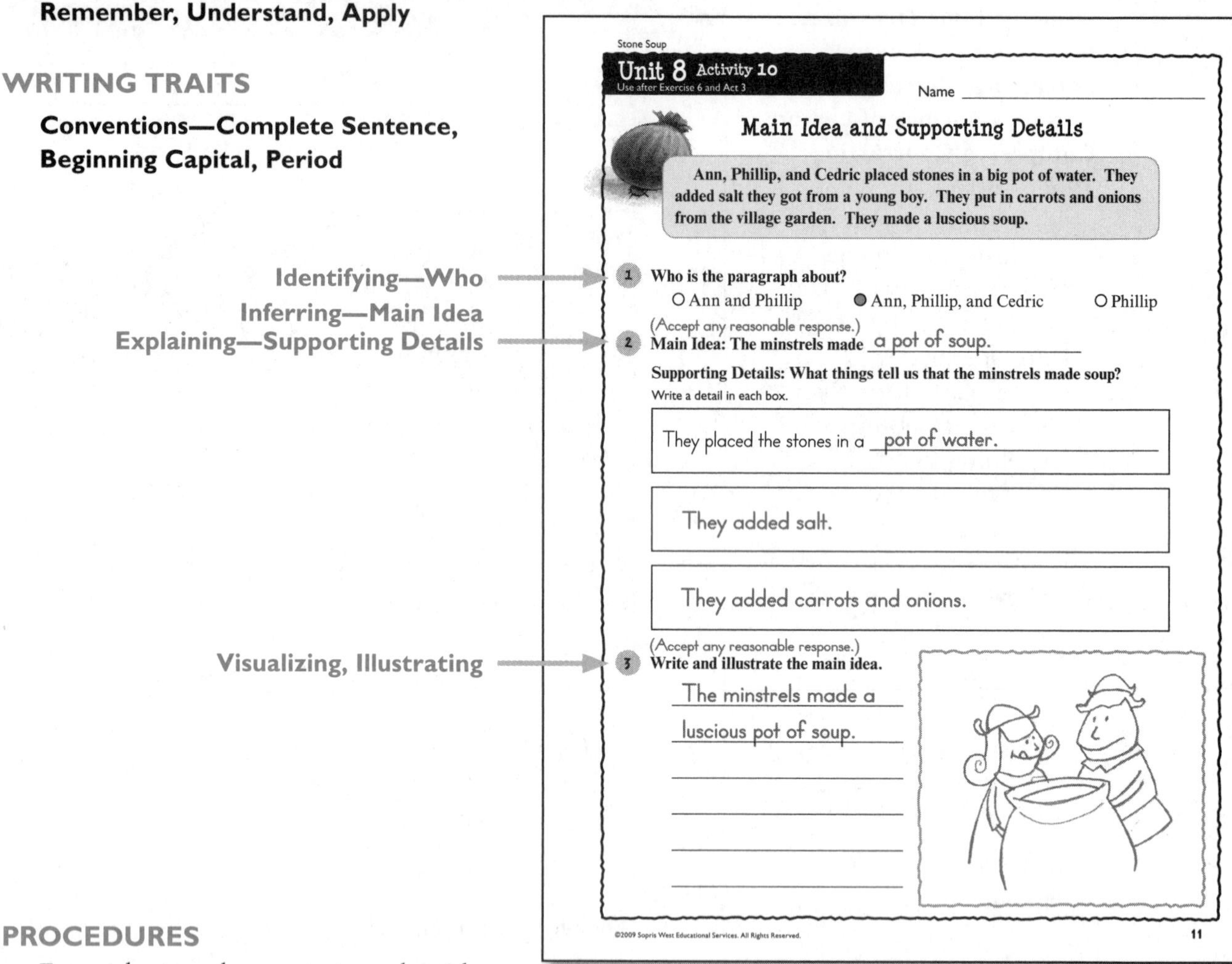

Identifying—Who
Inferring—Main Idea
Explaining—Supporting Details
Visualizing, Illustrating

Stone Soup

Unit 8 Activity 10
Use after Exercise 6 and Act 3

Name ____________

Main Idea and Supporting Details

Ann, Phillip, and Cedric placed stones in a big pot of water. They added salt they got from a young boy. They put in carrots and onions from the village garden. They made a luscious soup.

1 Who is the paragraph about?
○ Ann and Phillip ● Ann, Phillip, and Cedric ○ Phillip

(Accept any reasonable response.)
2 Main Idea: The minstrels made a pot of soup.

Supporting Details: What things tell us that the minstrels made soup?
Write a detail in each box.

They placed the stones in a pot of water.

They added salt.

They added carrots and onions.

(Accept any reasonable response.)
3 Write and illustrate the main idea.
The minstrels made a luscious pot of soup.

©2009 Sopris West Educational Services. All Rights Reserved. 11

PROCEDURES

For each step, demonstrate and guide practice, as needed. Then have students complete the page independently.

1. **Topic/Who: Selection Response—Basic Instructions** (Item 1)
   - Have students read the top paragraph.
   - Have students read the question and fill in the bubble with the correct answer.

2. **Main Idea/Supporting Details: Sentence Completion/Writing—Basic Instructions** (Item 2)
   - Have students read the main-idea sentence stem and fill in the blank to complete the sentence.
   - Have students read the supporting detail sentence stem and fill in the blank with a supporting detail from the paragraph.
   - Have students write an additional supporting detail from the paragraph in each box. Remind them to use a complete sentence with a capital and a period.

3. **Main Idea: Sentence Writing, Illustrating—Basic Instructions** (Item 3)
   Have students write the main-idea sentence. Remind them to use a capital and a period. Then have students draw a picture of the main idea.

FOLLOWING DIRECTIONS • MAKING STONE SOUP

COMPREHENSION PROCESSES

Remember, Understand, Evaluate

WRITING TRAITS

Conventions—Complete Sentence, Beginning Capital, Period

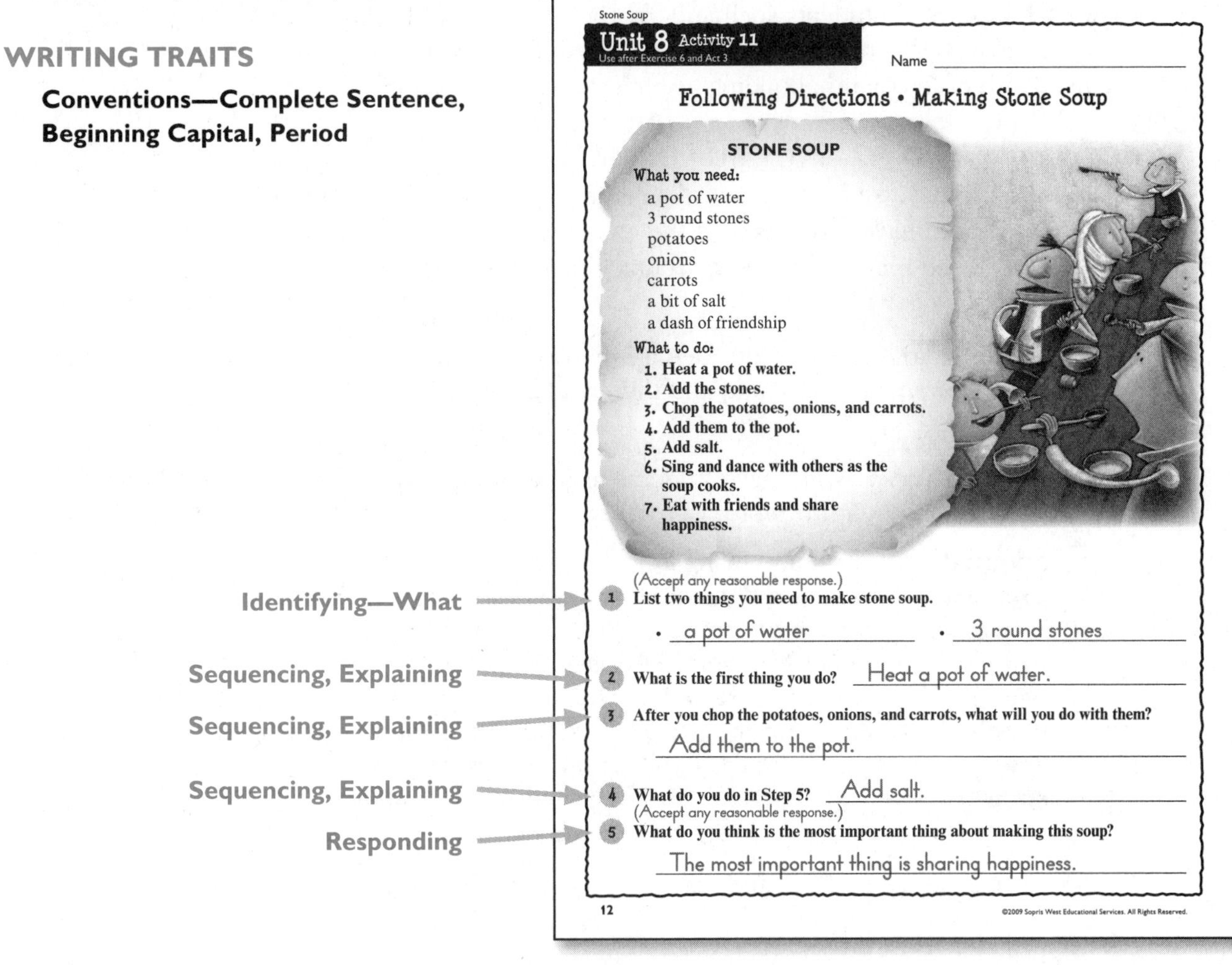

Stone Soup

Unit 8 Activity 11

Use after Exercise 6 and Act 3

Name ______________________

Following Directions • Making Stone Soup

STONE SOUP

What you need:

a pot of water
3 round stones
potatoes
onions
carrots
a bit of salt
a dash of friendship

What to do:

1. **Heat a pot of water.**
2. **Add the stones.**
3. **Chop the potatoes, onions, and carrots.**
4. **Add them to the pot.**
5. **Add salt.**
6. **Sing and dance with others as the soup cooks.**
7. **Eat with friends and share happiness.**

Identifying—What → (Accept any reasonable response.)
1 List two things you need to make stone soup.

• a pot of water • 3 round stones

Sequencing, Explaining → **2 What is the first thing you do?** Heat a pot of water.

Sequencing, Explaining → **3 After you chop the potatoes, onions, and carrots, what will you do with them?**

Add them to the pot.

Sequencing, Explaining → **4 What do you do in Step 5?** Add salt.

Responding → (Accept any reasonable response.)
5 What do you think is the most important thing about making this soup?

The most important thing is sharing happiness.

12

©2009 Sopris West Educational Services. All Rights Reserved.

PROCEDURES

For each step, demonstrate and guide practice, as needed. Then have students complete the page independently.

1. **Making Lists—Basic Instructions** (Item 1)
   - Have students read the directions and brainstorm possible answers.
   - Have students write the answers in the blanks.

2. **Sentence Writing—Basic Instructions** (Items 2–5)
   Have students read the questions and write complete sentence responses. Remind students to start with a capital and end with a period.

Self-monitoring

Have students check and correct their work.

❶ SOUND REVIEW

Have students read the sounds and key word phrases. Work for accuracy, then fluency.

❷ SOUND PRACTICE

- For each task, have students spell and say the focus sound in the gray bar. Next, have students read each underlined sound, the word, then the whole column.
- Repeat with each column, building accuracy first, then fluency.

❸ ACCURACY AND FLUENCY BUILDING

- For each task, have students say any underlined part, then read the word.
- Set a pace. Then have students read the whole words in each task and column.
- Provide repeated practice, building accuracy first, then fluency.

C1. Bossy E

For each word, have students identify the Bossy E on the end of the word. Have students identify the underlined sound and then read the word.

D1, E1. Tricky Words

- For each Tricky Word, have students use the sounds and word parts they know to silently sound out the word. Use the word in a sentence to help with pronunciation.

laughed Tom told a funny story. Everyone . . . *laughed.*
greatest I just read the best book ever. It was the . . . *greatest.*
lovely The flowers are . . . *lovely.*
boys Miriam had three children—one girl and two . . . *boys.*
brought We had a party with lots of food. Everyone . . . *brought* . . . something.
watch We're not going to play baseball today. We're just going to . . . *watch.*
shall It is raining and I can't go outside. What . . . *shall* . . . I do?
soup When Sheila is sick, her dad makes her chicken . . . *soup.*
water I am very thirsty. I want to drink some . . . *water.*

- Have students go back and read the whole words in the column.

❹ WORDS IN CONTEXT

For each word, have students use the sounds and word parts they know to silently sound out the word. Then have students read the sentence. Assist, as needed.

❺ MORPHOGRAPHS AND AFFIXES

- Have students read the underlined part, then the word.
- Repeat practice with whole words, mixing group and individual turns.
  Build accuracy, then fluency.

Stone Soup

Unit 8 Exercise 7

Use before rereading Acts 1–3

1. SOUND REVIEW Have students review sounds for accuracy, then for fluency.

A	-y as in baby	a as in ago	oo as in book	ce as in center	u_e as in flute
B	ir	ou	ay	-dge	igh

2. SOUND PRACTICE In each column, have students spell and say the sound, then say any underlined sound and the word. Next, have students read the whole column.

kn	ph	ci	aw
kneel know knew knife	graph phone trophy photo	circle pencil city circle	lawn squawked dawn dawdle

3. ACCURACY AND FLUENCY BUILDING For each column, have students say any underlined part, then read each word. Next, have students read the whole column.

A1 Mixed Review	B1 Mixed Review	C1 Bossy E	D1 Tricky Words	E1 Tricky Words
small smell bunch bench	rice race threw throw	ruled times lute square share	laughed greatest lovely boys	brought watch shall soup water

4. WORDS IN CONTEXT For each word, have students use the sounds and word parts they know to figure out the word. Then have them read the sentence.

A	med•i•cine	The doctor gave me medicine when I got sick.
B	char•ac•ter	Phillip is a main character in our story.

5. MORPHOGRAPHS AND AFFIXES Have students read each underlined word part, then the word.

drinkable	vacation	brightly	decided

9

TEACH TO MASTERY/ DISCRIMINATION PRACTICE

Repeated Practice (Reminder)

Provide repeated practice on each task. If you hear an error, gently correct the whole group with a demonstration and/or guided practice. Move to another skill or task, then return to the difficult item many times—mixing group and individual turns, independent of your voice. When a task is easy, build speed of recognition.

Remember, practice makes perfect! And practice builds fluency.

STONE SOUP ACTS 1–3 INSTRUCTIONS

Students reread the entire play with the teacher. Have fun! Set up a tape recorder or video camera. Use a karaoke machine. Invite a few visitors or take your play on the road with a visit to the front office and the principal.

PROCEDURES

1. **Getting Started**
   - Assign roles. (See pages 56 and 57 of this teacher's guide.)
   - Give each student a placard identifying his or her part.
     Include the following sentence stem:
     Hi, my name is [Jennifer Matsumoto]. I am in second grade. My part is [Narrator 1].
   - Rehearse the first act, then let the performance commence.

2. **Act 1**
   - Let each student introduce himself or herself using the following sentence pattern.
     Hi, my name is [Joseph Jackson]. I am in second grade. My part is [Narrator 1].
   - Have students read their parts.
   - Between Acts 2 and 3, debrief the performance.

3. **Acts 2 and 3**
   Have students read their parts.

4. **Optional Fun Activity**
   If you've tape recorded the session, let students listen to the tape outside of the reading block.

5. **Written Assessment (Comprehension and Skill)**
   Tell students they will do a Written Assessment after they read "Stone Soup." For teacher directions, see pages 101 and 102.

6. **Homework, Comprehension and Skill 8: Repeated Reading**

WRITTEN ASSESSMENT

COMPREHENSION PROCESSES

Remember, Understand, Apply

WRITING TRAITS

Conventions—Complete Sentence, Capital, Period
Presentation

Test Taking

Identifying—Main Character
Sentence Writing

Identifying—Beginning, Initiating Event

Identifying—Middle, Action

Inferring—End

Inferring; Explaining
Using Vocabulary—bittersweet
Sentence Completion

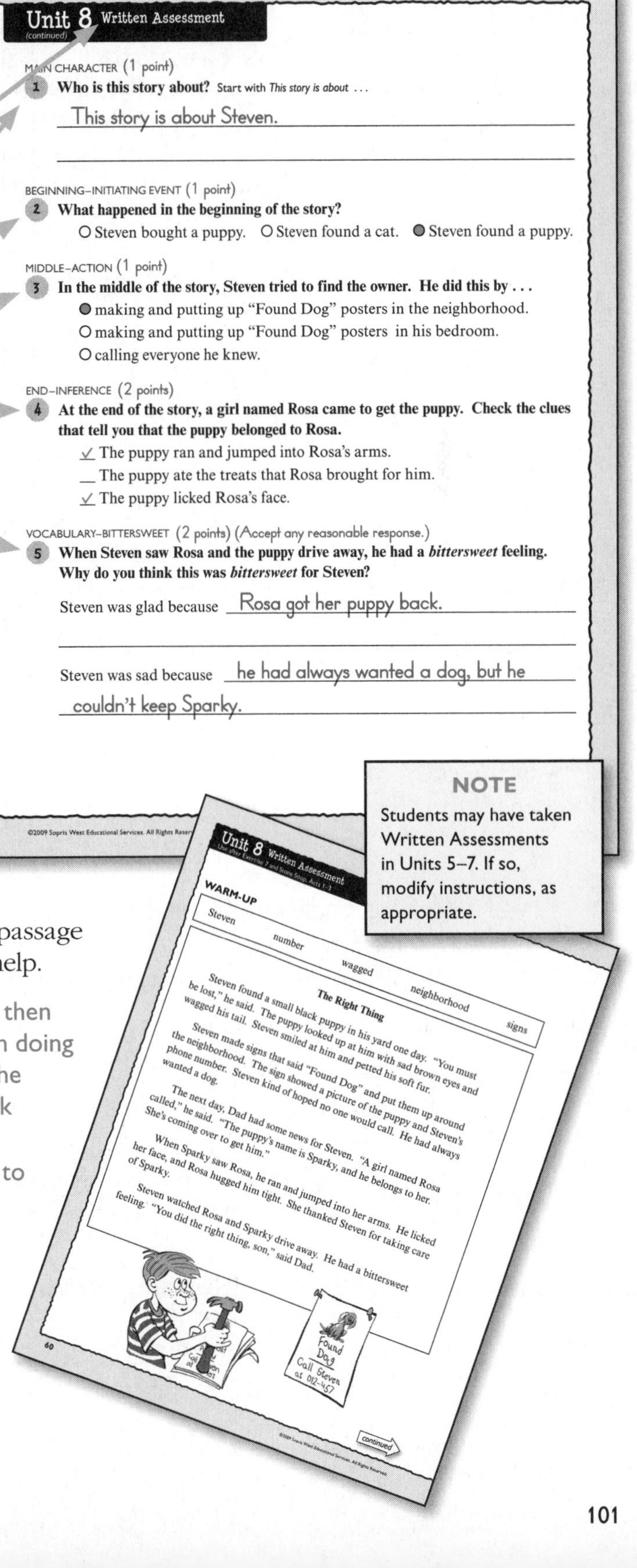

Unit 8 Written Assessment (continued)

MAIN CHARACTER (1 point)

1 **Who is this story about?** Start with *This story is about ...*

This story is about Steven.

BEGINNING–INITIATING EVENT (1 point)

2 **What happened in the beginning of the story?**

○ Steven bought a puppy. ○ Steven found a cat. ● Steven found a puppy.

MIDDLE–ACTION (1 point)

3 **In the middle of the story, Steven tried to find the owner. He did this by . . .**

● making and putting up "Found Dog" posters in the neighborhood.
○ making and putting up "Found Dog" posters in his bedroom.
○ calling everyone he knew.

END–INFERENCE (2 points)

4 **At the end of the story, a girl named Rosa came to get the puppy. Check the clues that tell you that the puppy belonged to Rosa.**

✓ The puppy ran and jumped into Rosa's arms.
__ The puppy ate the treats that Rosa brought for him.
✓ The puppy licked Rosa's face.

VOCABULARY–BITTERSWEET (2 points) (Accept any reasonable response.)

5 **When Steven saw Rosa and the puppy drive away, he had a *bittersweet* feeling. Why do you think this was *bittersweet* for Steven?**

Steven was glad because Rosa got her puppy back.

Steven was sad because he had always wanted a dog, but he couldn't keep Sparky.

Unit 8 Written Assessment

WARM-UP

Steven number wagged neighborhood signs

The Right Thing

Steven found a small black puppy in his yard one day. "You must be lost," he said. The puppy looked up at him with sad brown eyes and wagged his tail. Steven smiled at him and petted his soft fur.

Steven made signs that said "Found Dog" and put them up around the neighborhood. The sign showed a picture of the puppy and Steven's phone number. Steven kind of hoped no one would call. He had always wanted a dog.

The next day, Dad had some news for Steven. "A girl named Rosa called," he said. "The puppy's name is Sparky, and he belongs to her. She's coming over to get him."

When Sparky saw Rosa, he ran and jumped into her arms. He licked her face, and Rosa hugged him tight. She thanked Steven for taking care of Sparky.

Steven watched Rosa and Sparky drive away. He had a bittersweet feeling. "You did the right thing, son," said Dad.

60

continued

NOTE

Students may have taken Written Assessments in Units 5–7. If so, modify instructions, as appropriate.

PROCEDURES

Do not demonstrate or guide practice.

Written Assessment—Introductory Instructions

1. Introduce the Written Assessment.
   - Remind students that their work today is an opportunity for them to show what they can do independently.
   - Tell students they will whisper read the passage and then answer the questions without help.

You're going to whisper read a passage and then answer the questions—just like you've been doing on your Comprehension and Skill Work. The only thing different is that you need to work by yourself.

If you read a question and aren't sure what to do, reread the question and try again.

What should you do if you can't answer a question? (Reread the question and try again.)

If you still can't answer the question, reread the passage and try again.

What should you do if you still can't answer a question?
(Reread the passage and try again.)

If you still aren't sure, just do your best.

WRITTEN ASSESSMENT (*continued*)

Inferring—Character Traits (Characterization)
Using Vocabulary—integrity

Unit 8 Written Assessment
(continued)

CHARACTERIZATION, VOCABULARY–INTEGRITY (1 point)

6 **Steven's actions showed that he had *integrity*. Explain how Steven showed *integrity*.**

- ○ Steven gave the puppy to the pet store.
- ○ Steven kept the puppy.
- ● Steven tried to find the owner of the puppy.

✓ Check and Correct

Reread your answers.
Do your answers make sense? ☑
Do you have a capital at the beginning of each sentence and a period at the end? ☑
Did you use your best handwriting? ☑

SCORING Date ______

Main Character 1 /1	Beginning 1 /1	Middle 1 /1	
End 2 /2	Vocabulary 2 /2	Characterization 1 /1	Total 8 /8

Teachers: If you wish to keep a cumulative record of student assessment scores, see the *Assessment Manual.*

62

©2009 Sopris West Educational Services. All Rights Reserved.

2. Check for student understanding.
   Say something like:
   Look at your assessment. What are you going to do first? (Write my name.)

   What are going to do next? (Whisper read the passage.)
   What will you do after you read the passage? (Answer the questions.)

   That's great. Now what will you do if you get to a hard question?
   (Reread the question and try again.)
   That's right. What should you do if it's still hard? (Reread the passage and try again.)
   Very good. And if you still aren't sure, what will you do? (Do my best and keep going.)

3. Remind students to check and correct.
   When you finish your assessment, what should you do? (Check and correct.)
   That's right. Go to the top of the page. Reread the questions and make sure your answers make sense. Fix anything that doesn't sound right. Make sure you have an answer for every question.

4. Remind students what to do when they finish their work.

End of the Unit

In this section, you will find:

Making Decisions

As you near the end of the unit, plan to give the Written Assessment and the Oral Reading Fluency Assessment to each child in your group. Use this section as a general guide for making instructional decisions and doing diagnostic planning.

Written Assessment

The Unit 8 Written Assessment is located on page 60 of the activity book and on the CD.

Oral Reading Fluency Assessment

The Unit 8 Oral Reading Fluency Assessment is located on page 107 of this teacher's guide and in the *Assessment Manual.*

Certificate of Achievement

Celebrate your children's accomplishments. When your students master the unit skills, send home the Certificate of Achievement.

Goal Setting

Have students set goals for the next unit.

Extra Practice Lessons

Use the Extra Practice lessons for students who need additional decoding and fluency work. Student materials can be copied from the Extra Practice blackline masters.

Making Decisions

GENERAL ASSESSMENT GUIDELINES

1. After students complete Story Reading 7, a rereading of "Stone Soup," give the group the Unit 8 Written Assessment in place of Comprehension and Skill Work. Follow the instructions on pages 101 and 102 of this guide.

2. While the group is completing the Written Assessment or any time during the day, administer the Oral Reading Fluency Assessment. Assess each student individually.

   Optional: Graph the results of the assessment. (See Unit 7 Teacher's Guide, pages 92 and 95.)
   - If the student's words correct per minute go up, congratulate the student.
   - If the student's words correct per minute go down, discuss the student's overall improvement and help him or her identify ways to improve for the next assessment.

3. Score oral fluency responses on the Student Assessment Record. Adhere to the scoring criteria in the *Assessment Manual.* Use a stopwatch to time how long it takes each student to read the Oral Reading Fluency Passage, and record errors.

USING THE WRITTEN ASSESSMENT RESULTS

Results of the Written Assessment *should not* be used to determine whether a student or group of students continues forward in the program. As long as students pass the Oral Reading Fluency Assessment, they should continue forward with the next unit.

The Written Assessment should be used to informally monitor how well students read independently and answer questions in writing. If any student has difficulty with the Written Assessment, re-administer the assessment orally.

If the student has difficulty answering the questions orally:
- Record the types of errors (e.g., main idea, sequencing, open-ended response).
- Provide explicit instruction for these types of questions during reading group, before independent work, and in tutorials, as needed.
  1) Demonstrate (or model) appropriate responses, guide practice, and provide opportunities for independent practice.
  2) For inferential questions, think aloud with students—explain how you arrive at an answer.
  3) For literal questions, teach students to reread a passage, locate information, reread the question, and respond.

At this level, if the student is able to answer the questions orally but not on paper, it may not be due to comprehension problems. The student's difficulties may be related to a lack of motivation, an inability to work independently, or a struggle with handwriting, spelling, language, or vocabulary.

USING THE ORAL READING FLUENCY RESULTS

At the end of each unit, you will need to make decisions regarding student progress. Should students go forward in the program? Does the group need Extra Practice before proceeding? Do individuals require more assistance and practice to continue working in their group? These decisions all require use of the oral reading fluency data and professional judgment. As you analyze assessment results, watch for trends and anomalies.

See the *Assessment Manual* for detailed information and instructional recommendations. General guidelines and recommendations follow:

Strong Pass ≥ 107 WCPM 0–2 errors	• Continue with the current pace of instruction. • Have students set goals. (Until students are reading approximately 180 words correct per minute, oral reading fluency continues to be an instructional goal.)
Pass 86–106 WCPM 0–2 errors	• Continue with the current pace of instruction. Consider increasing fluency practice.
No Pass ≤ 85 WCPM RED FLAG A No Pass is a red flag. A mild early intervention can prevent an intense and time-consuming intervention in the future.	• If a child scores a No Pass but has previously passed all assessments, you may wish to advance the student to the next unit, then carefully monitor the student. • If a child scores a No Pass but has previously passed all assessments, you may wish to advance the student to the next unit and also provide additional practice opportunities. (See below.) • If a child scores two consecutive No Passes or periodic No Passes, additional practice must be provided. (See below.) • If a child scores three consecutive No Passes, the student should be placed in a lower-performing group.

Added Practice Options for Groups

Warm-Ups:

- Begin each lesson with Partner Reading of the previous day's homework.
- Begin each day with Partner Reading of a Word Fluency from Extra Practice.
- Begin each lesson with a five-minute Fluency Booster. Place copies of Units 1–7 *Read Well* Homework in three-ring notebooks. Each day, have students begin Finger Tracking and Whisper Reading at Unit 1, Homework 1. At the end of five minutes, have students mark where they are in their notebooks. The next day, the goal is to read farther.
- Begin each Story Reading with a review of the previous day's story.
- After reading the story, include Short Passage Practice on a daily basis.

Extended Units: If several children begin to score No Passes or barely pass, extend the unit by adding Extra Practices 1, 2, and/or 3. Extra Practice lessons include Decoding Practice, Fluency Passage, Word Fluency, and a Comprehension and Skill Activity. (See pages 110–121 in this guide.)

Jell-Well Reviews: A Jell-Well Review is the *Read Well* term for a review of earlier units. A Jell-Well Review is a period of time taken to celebrate what children have learned and an opportunity to firm up their foundation of learning. To complete a Jell-Well Review, take the group back to the last unit for which all students scored Strong Passes. Then quickly cycle back up. See the *Assessment Manual* for how to build a Jell-Well Review.

Added Practice Options for Individual Students

Tutorials: Set up five-minute tutorials on a daily basis with an assistant, trained volunteer, or cross-age tutor. Have the tutor provide Short Passage Practice and Timed Readings or Extra Practice lessons.

Double Dose: Find ways to provide a double dose of *Read Well* instruction.

- Have the student work in his or her group *and* a lower-performing group.
- Have an instructional assistant, older student, or parent volunteer preview or review lessons.
- Have an instructional assistant provide instruction with Extra Practice lessons.
- Preview new lessons or review previous lessons.

END-OF-THE-UNIT CELEBRATION

When students pass the Oral Reading Fluency Assessment, celebrate with the Certificate of Achievement on p. 108.

Note: Using the Flesch-Kincaid Grade Level readability formula, the Unit 8 Assessment has a 2.4 readability level. Readability formulas provide only a rough estimate of difficulty. Just adding one or two multisyllabic words to the passage can increase the readability by one or two months.

GOAL SETTING

If you choose to have students set goals, help them brainstorm accomplishments in reading.

Say something like:

Let's look at our goal-setting form.
Read the top part with me.
(In this unit, I learned about folktales. I can read . . .)

My Goals

In this unit, I learned about folktales. I can read big words like integrity and appreciate. I also read a part in our wonderful performance of the play "Stone Soup."

My goal for Unit 9 is 94 words correct per minute.

I can work to reach my goal by:

- Reading and rereading carefully
- Working hard in reading group
- Listening to others read

Signed Jonathan

Date Nov. 1

My Personal Best:

In Unit 8, I read 93 words correct per minute.

Since the beginning of the year, I've improved my reading by 10 words per minute.

That's a great accomplishment.
It is something to be proud of!
Look at the next line. It shows your goal for Unit 9.

The next line says, "I can work to reach my goal by . . . "
Everyone, read the dots. How can you work to reach your goal?
(reading and rereading carefully, working hard in reading group . . .)

[Jonathan], how will you work to reach your goal? (listening to others read)

The box with the birds tells you what your fluency was for Unit 8. It also tells how much your reading has improved since the beginning of the year. I'm impressed by how much everyone has improved!

TRICKY WORD and FOCUS SKILL WARM-UP

know	Ralph	delicious	phone	taught	curious

ORAL READING FLUENCY PASSAGE

Phillip's Soup

★It was a cold winter day. We were hungry. "What	10
should we make for dinner?" asked Mom.	17
Phillip said, "I know how to make stone soup. Our	27
teacher taught us how to make it."	34
Mom heated a pot of water. Phillip chopped onions, and	44
Dad threw in some carrots. Then we decided to add some ham,	56
corn, and rice.	59
The soup began to smell so good that we decided to share	71
it with our friends. Mom went to the phone and invited some of	84
them to dinner. They were curious about the soup.	93
Soon everyone but Ralph had gathered at our house.	102
When the phone rang, Ralph said he would be here soon.	113
We waited and waited. When Ralph finally arrived, we	122
were all very hungry. The soup was delicious. We ate, laughed,	133
and had a great time together.	139

ORAL READING FLUENCY Start timing at the ★. Mark errors. Make a single slash in the text (/) at 60 seconds. If the student completes the passage in less than 60 seconds, have the student go back to the ★ and continue reading. Make a double slash (//) in the text at 60 seconds.

WCPM Determine words correct per minute by subtracting errors from words read in 60 seconds.

STRONG PASS The student scores no more than 2 errors on the first pass through the passage and reads 107 or more words correct per minute. Proceed to Unit 9.

PASS The student scores no more than 2 errors on the first pass through the passage and reads 86 to 106 words correct per minute. Proceed to Unit 9.

NO PASS The student scores 3 or more errors on the first pass through the passage and/or reads 85 or fewer words correct per minute. Provide added fluency practice with *RW2* Unit 8 Extra Practice. (Lessons and BLMs follow the certificate at the end of the teacher's guide.) After completing the Extra Practice, retest the student.

Wonderful Work!

____

has successfully completed

Read Well* 2 Unit 8 • *Traditional Tales

with ______ words correct per minute.

Teacher Signature __________________________

Date ___________________________________

Wonderful Work!

____

has successfully completed

Read Well* 2 Unit 8 • *Traditional Tales

with ______ words correct per minute.

Teacher Signature __________________________

Date ___________________________________

My Goals

In this unit, I learned about folktales. I can read big words like integrity and appreciate. I also read a part in our wonderful performance of the play "Stone Soup."

My goal for Unit 9 is _____ words correct per minute.

I can work to reach my goal by:

- Reading and rereading carefully
- Working hard in reading group
- ______________________________
  ____

Signed ______________________________

Date ______________________________

My Personal Best:

In Unit 8, I read _____ words correct per minute.

Since the beginning of the year, I've improved my reading by ______ words per minute.

My Goals

In this unit, I learned about folktales. I can read big words like integrity and appreciate. I also read a part in our wonderful performance of the play "Stone Soup."

My goal for Unit 9 is _____ words correct per minute.

I can work to reach my goal by:

- Reading and rereading carefully
- Working hard in reading group
- ______________________________
  ____

Signed ______________________________

Date ______________________________

My Personal Best:

In Unit 8, I read _____ words correct per minute.

Since the beginning of the year, I've improved my reading by ______ words per minute.

PROCEDURES

CAUTION

Your children may not need Extra Practice. Use assessment results to determine if Extra Practice is needed.

1. Sound Review

Use selected Sound Cards from Units 1–8.

2. Sounding Out Smoothly

- For each word, have students say the underlined part, sound out the word smoothly, then read the whole word. (Use the words in sentences, as needed.)
- Have students read all the words in the row, building accuracy first, then fluency.
- Repeat practice. Mix group and individual turns, independent of your voice.

3. Accuracy and Fluency Building

- For each task, have students say any underlined part, then read each word.
- Set a pace. Then have students read the whole words in each task and column.
- Provide repeated practice, building accuracy first, then fluency.

4. Tricky Words

Have students read each row for accuracy, then read the entire grid for fluency.

5. Multisyllabic Words

For each word, have students read each syllable out loud, finger count the syllables, then tell how many syllables are in the word. If needed, use the word in a sentence. Have students read the whole word.

6. Dictation

teach, peach, speech, say, may, tray

- Say "teach." Have students say the word. Guide students as they finger count and say the sounds. Have students touch or write the sounds, then read the word. Say something like:

  The first word is ***teach.*** Say the word. (teach)
  Say and count the sounds in ***teach*** with me.

  Hold up one finger for each sound. /t/•/ēēē/•/ch/ How many sounds? (three)

  What's the first sound? (/t/) Touch under /t/.
  What's the next sound? (/ēēē/) Write /ēēē/ with the e-a pattern.
  What's the last sound? (/ch/) Touch under /ch/.
  Read the word. (teach)

- Repeat with "peach" and "speech."
- Continue with the rhyming words: say, may, tray.

EXTRA PRACTICE 1

Unit 8 Decoding Practice

Name ______________________________

1. SOUND REVIEW Use selected Sound Cards from Units 1–8.

2. SOUNDING OUT SMOOTHLY Have students say the underlined part, sound out and read each word, then read the row.

hard	face	silk	sleeve

3. ACCURACY/FLUENCY BUILDING Have students say any underlined part, then read each word. Next, have students read the column.

A1 Sound Practice	B1 Word Endings	C1 Tricky Words With Endings	D1 Tricky Word Buildups
Phillip Ralph know knew **A2** Mixed Practice garden tattered morning hungry	kindness dirty asked looked prune pruning chop chopped hot hotter	working pulling watching **C2** Bossy E ate robe wore tired wiped	point appoint disappoint **D2** Tricky Words appreciate curious delicious scrumptious

4. TRICKY WORDS Have students read each row for accuracy, then fluency.

A	soup	taught	onions	laughed	brought	5
B	clothes	one	were	some	work	10

5. MULTISYLLABIC WORDS Have students read the word by parts, tell how many syllables are in the word, then read the whole word.

A	sum•mer	summer	win•ter	winter
B	splen•did	spendid	fin•al•ly	finally
C	em•bar•rassed	embarrassed	Em•per•or	Emperor

6. DICTATION Say the word. Have students say the word, then finger count and say the sounds. Have students say each sound as they touch or write it.

A1 Shifty Words	B1 Rhyming Words
t e a ch p ea ch s p ee ch	s a y m a y t r a y

PROCEDURES

1. **First Reading**
   Mix group and individual turns, independent of your voice. Have students work toward an accuracy goal of 0–2 errors and practice any difficult words.

2. **Second Reading, Short Passage Practice: Developing Prosody**
   - Demonstrate how to read a line or two with expression. Read at a rate slightly faster than the students' rate. Say something like:
     Listen as I read the first two sentences with expression and phrasing. I'm going to emphasize certain words and pause between sentences.
     "One summer morning, Jun and his grandfather were pruning the trees in the Emperor's garden. As the day went on, Jun got hotter and hotter."
   - Guide practice with your voice.
     Now read the paragraph with me.
   - Provide individual turns while others track with their fingers and whisper read. Provide descriptive and positive feedback.
     [Nikolas], you read with wonderful expression!

EXTRA PRACTICE 1

Unit 8 Fluency Passage

Name ______________________

Fluency Passage

My goal is to read with 0–2 errors and ___ words correct per minute.

I read with ___ errors and ___ words correct per minute.

An Act of Kindness

One summer morning, Jun and his grandfather were pruning the	10
trees in the Emperor's garden. As the day went on, Jun got hotter and	24
hotter. He wiped his face on his sleeve. He drank some water. It was	38
hard to keep working. But he didn't want to disappoint his grandfather.	50
Jun was pulling weeds when he looked up and saw the Emperor	62
watching him work. Jun was embarrassed. He was dirty and tired, and	74
his clothes were tattered.	78
The Emperor wore a splendid silk robe and held a tray of food. "Are	92
you hungry?" asked the Emperor. "I've brought lunch for you and your	104
grandfather. I appreciate your hard work."	110
Jun was speechless. Finally he said, "Thank you!" Jun and his	121
grandfather sat and ate the scrumptious meal.	128

Homework
I've listened to my child read this passage twice. Date ________ Signed ______________

56

3. **Partner Reading: Repeated Reading (Checkout Opportunity)**

While students do Partner Reading, listen to individuals read the passage. Work on accuracy and fluency, as needed.

4. **Homework: Repeated Reading**

Have students read the story at home.

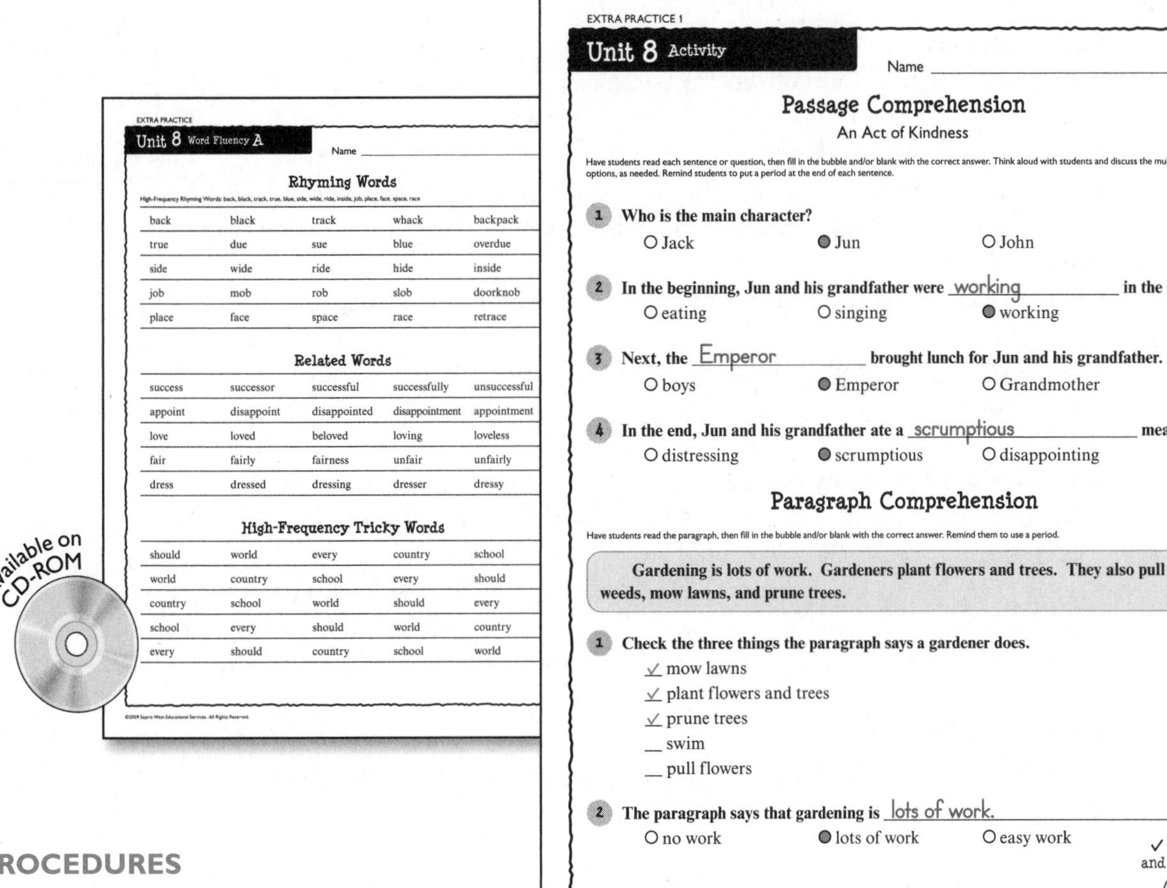
EXTRA PRACTICE

Unit 8 Word Fluency A

Name

Rhyming Words

back	black	track	whack	backpack
true	due	sue	blue	overdue
side	wide	ride	hide	inside
job	mob	rob	slob	doorknob
place	face	space	race	retrace

Related Words

success	successor	successful	successfully	unsuccessful
appoint	disappoint	disappointed	disappointment	appointment
love	loved	beloved	loving	loveless
fair	fairly	fairness	unfair	unfairly
dress	dressed	dressing	dresser	dressy

High-Frequency Tricky Words

should	world	every	country	school
world	country	school	every	should
country	school	world	should	every
school	every	should	world	country
every	should	country	school	world

EXTRA PRACTICE 1

Unit 8 Activity

Name

Passage Comprehension

An Act of Kindness

Have students read each sentence or question, then fill in the bubble and/or blank with the correct answer. Think aloud with students and discuss the multiple-choice options, as needed. Remind students to put a period at the end of each sentence.

1. Who is the main character?
   ○ Jack ● Jun ○ John
2. In the beginning, Jun and his grandfather were working in the garden.
   ○ eating ○ singing ● working
3. Next, the Emperor brought lunch for Jun and his grandfather.
   ○ boys ● Emperor ○ Grandmother
4. In the end, Jun and his grandfather ate a scrumptious meal.
   ○ distressing ● scrumptious ○ disappointing

Paragraph Comprehension

Have students read the paragraph, then fill in the bubble and/or blank with the correct answer. Remind them to use a period.

Gardening is lots of work. Gardeners plant flowers and trees. They also pull weeds, mow lawns, and prune trees.

1. Check the three things the paragraph says a gardener does.
   ✓ mow lawns
   ✓ plant flowers and trees
   ✓ prune trees
   __ swim
   __ pull flowers
2. The paragraph says that gardening is lots of work.
   ○ no work ● lots of work ○ easy work

✓ Check and Correct

 57

PROCEDURES

For each step, demonstrate and guide practice, as needed. Then have students complete the page independently.

1. Activity

Passage Comprehension

- Have students read each sentence or question, then fill in the bubble and/or blank with the correct answer.
- Think aloud with students and discuss the multiple-choice options, as needed.

Paragraph Comprehension

- Have students read the paragraph.
- Have students read each numbered sentence, then fill in the bubble and/or blank or check the correct answer.
- Have students read the completed sentence.

Self-monitoring

Have students read and check their work, then draw a happy face in the Check and Correct circle.

2. Word Fluency (BLMs are located on the CD.)

- To build fluency, have students read Rhyming Words, Related Words, and High-Frequency Tricky Words. Have students read each section three times in a row.
- To build accuracy, have students read all sets with partners.

> **ACCURACY BEFORE FLUENCY (Reminder)**
>
> Word Fluency is designed to build accuracy and fluency. Students should practice for accuracy before working on fluency.

> **CAUTION**
> Your children may not need Extra Practice. Use assessment results to determine if Extra Practice is needed.

PROCEDURES

1. Sound Review

Use selected Sound Cards from Units 1–8.

2. Sounding Out Smoothly

- For each word, have students say the underlined part, sound out the word smoothly, then read the whole word. (Use the words in sentences, as needed.)
- Have students read all the words in the row, building accuracy first, then fluency.
- Repeat practice. Mix group and individual turns, independent of your voice.

3. Accuracy and Fluency Building

- For each task, have students say any underlined part, then read each word.
- Set a pace. Then have students read the whole words in each task and column.
- Provide repeated practice, building accuracy first, then fluency.

4. Tricky Words

Have students read each row for accuracy, then read the entire grid for fluency.

5. Multisyllabic Words

For each word, have students read each syllable out loud, finger count the syllables, then tell how many syllables are in the word. If needed, use the word in a sentence. Have students read the whole word.

6. Dictation

ring, rang, sang, play, sway, tray

- Say "ring." Have students say the word. Guide students as they finger count and say the sounds. Have students touch or write the sounds, then read the word.

  The first word is ***ring.*** Say the word. (ring)
  Say and count the sounds in ***ring*** with me.

  Hold up one finger for each sound. /rrr/•/ĭĭĭ/•/nnn/•/g/ How many sounds? (four)

  What's the first sound? (/rrr/) Touch under /rrr/.
  What's the next sound? (/ĭĭĭ/) Write /ĭĭĭ/.
  What's the next sound? (/nnn/) Touch under /nnn/.
  What's the last sound? (/g/) Touch under /g/.
  Read the word. (ring)

- Repeat with "rang" and "sang."
- Continue with the rhyming words: play, sway, tray.

EXTRA PRACTICE 2

Unit 8 Decoding Practice

Name ______________________

1. SOUND REVIEW Use selected Sound Cards from Units 1–8.

2. SOUNDING OUT SMOOTHLY Have students say the underlined part, sound out and read each word, then read the row.

know	phone	Ralph	threw

3. ACCURACY/FLUENCY BUILDING Have students say any underlined part, then read each word. Next, have students read the column.

A1 Sound Practice	B1 Word Endings	C1 Bossy E	D1 Buildups
along across about **A2** Mixed Practice heated waited played plenty	cry cried tap tapped dance dancing **B2** Contractions have not haven't	lute tune whole square stone decided smiled invited arrived	cord record recorder car care scare scarce appear appeared

4. TRICKY WORDS Have students read each row for accuracy, then fluency.

A	taught	music	quiet	woman	heard	5
B	exhausted	merry	spread	curious	laughed	10

5. MULTISYLLABIC WORDS Have students read the word by parts, tell how many syllables are in the word, then read the whole word.

A	Phil•lip	Phillip	Ced•ric	Cedric
B	min•strels	minstrels	car•rots	carrots
C	vil•la•gers	villagers	won•der•ful	wonderful

6. DICTATION Say the word. Have students say the word, then finger count and say the sounds. Have students say each sound as they touch or write it.

A1 Shifty Words	B1 Rhyming Words
r i n g r a n g s a n g	p l a y s w a y t r a y

58

PROCEDURES

EXTRA PRACTICE 2

Unit 8 Fluency Passage

Name ____________

Fluency Passage

My goal is to read with 0–2 errors and ___ words correct per minute.

I read with ___ errors and ___ words correct per minute.

Bring On the Music

After walking for days, three minstrels came to a village. The village	12
seemed sad and quiet.	16
"Why is it so quiet here?" Phillip asked an old woman. "Are you sad?	30
Is food scarce?"	33
"We have plenty of food," said the woman. "But we haven't heard	45
music in years. There is no dancing." So Ann got out her recorder, and	59
Cedric picked up his lute. They played a merry tune, and Phillip sang	72
along with them.	75
The old woman began to sway, and a smile slowly spread across her	88
face. Curious villagers appeared in the square. They tapped a beat,	99
smiled, and laughed. Soon the whole village was dancing.	108
"Oh, what a wonderful time!" cried the old woman. "We will have	120
a splendid meal. Then we will dance to your music until we are all	134
exhausted!"	135
And so they did.	139

Homework
I've listened to my child read this passage twice. Date ________ Signed ____________

59

1. **First Reading**
   Mix group and individual turns, independent of your voice. Have students work toward an accuracy goal of 0–2 errors and practice any difficult words.

2. **Second Reading, Timed Reading: Repeated Reading**

   - Once the group accuracy goal has been achieved, time individual students for 30 or 60 seconds while the other children track with their fingers and whisper read.
   - Determine words correct per minute. Record student scores. Celebrate when students reach their goals!

     Wow! [Akemi], you met your goal. That was your best score ever. You get to read to the principal this week.

3. **Partner Reading: Repeated Reading (Checkout Opportunity)**

   While students do Partner Reading, listen to individuals read the passage. Work on accuracy and fluency, as needed.

4. **Homework: Repeated Reading**

   Have students read the story at home.

EXTRA PRACTICE

Unit 8 Word Fluency B

Name ______________

Rhyming Words

High-Frequency Rhyming Words: ice, cool, school, show, grow, low, snow, follow, air, pair, hair, fair, well, spell, tell, fell

spice	ice	price	mice	entice
fool	cool	school	tool	whirlpool
show	grow	low	snow	follow
air	pair	hair	fair	repair
well	spell	tell	fell	seashell

Related Words

wonder	wondered	wondering	wonderful	wonderfully
surprise	surprised	surprising	surprisingly	surprises
honor	honest	honesty	dishonest	dishonor
wrap	wrapped	wrapping	wrapper	unwrapped
narrate	narrated	narrating	narrator	narration

High-Frequency Tricky Words

father	earth	eye	thought	don't
earth	father	thought	don't	eye
eye	don't	father	earth	thought
thought	eye	don't	father	earth
don't	thought	earth	eye	father

Available on CD-ROM

EXTRA PRACTICE 2

Unit 8 Activity

Name ______________

Passage Comprehension

Bring On the Music

Have students read each sentence or question, then fill in the bubble and/or blank with the correct answer. Think aloud with students and discuss the multiple-choice options, as needed.

1. **Who came to the village?**
   - ○ a woman ● three minstrels ○ villagers
2. **In the beginning, the village was quiet because . . .**
   - ○ the villagers did not have food. ● the villagers had not heard music in years.
3. **In the middle, the minstrels played music. What did the villagers start to do?**
   - ○ run ○ walk ● dance
4. **In the end, the villagers danced until they were exhausted. This means that they danced until they were . . .**
   - ● very tired. ○ very happy. ○ very big.

Paragraph Comprehension

Have students read the paragraph, then fill in the bubble and/or blank with the correct answer. Remind them to use a period.

The minstrels played music and sang for a long time. Ann played the recorder, Cedric played the lute, and Phillip sang. They had fun playing music and singing until they were exhausted.

1. **The minstrels played and sang** for a long time.
   - ○ for only a short time ● for a long time
2. **Check what the minstrels did.**
   - ✓ Ann played the recorder. __ Phillip played the drums.
   - ✓ Cedric played the lute. ✓ Phillip sang.
3. **The minstrels played until they were** exhausted.
   - ○ distressed ● exhausted ○ disappointed

✓ Check and Correct ☺

 60

PROCEDURES

For each step, demonstrate and guide practice, as needed. Then have students complete the page independently.

1. Activity

Passage Comprehension

- Have students read each sentence or question, then fill in the bubble with the correct answer.
- Think aloud with students and discuss the multiple-choice options, as needed.

Paragraph Comprehension

- Have students read the paragraph.
- Have students read each numbered sentence or sentence stem, then fill in the bubble and/or blank, or check the correct anwer.
- Have students read the completed sentences.

Self-monitoring

Have students read and check their work, then draw a happy face in the Check and Correct circle.

2. Word Fluency (BLMs are located on the CD.)

- To build fluency, have students read Rhyming Words, Related Words, and High-Frequency Tricky Words. Have students read each section three times in a row.
- To build accuracy, have students read all sets with partners.

ACCURACY BEFORE FLUENCY
(Reminder)

Word Fluency is designed to build accuracy and fluency. Students should practice for accuracy before working on fluency.

PROCEDURES

> **CAUTION**
> Your children may not need Extra Practice. Use assessment results to determine if Extra Practice is needed.

1. Sound Review

Use selected Sound Cards from Units 1–8.

2. Sounding Out Smoothly

- For each word, have students say the underlined part, sound out the word smoothly, then read the whole word. (Use the words in sentences, as needed.)
- Have students read all the words in the row, building accuracy first, then fluency.
- Repeat practice. Mix group and individual turns, independent of your voice.

3. Accuracy and Fluency Building

- For each task, have students say any underlined part, then read each word.
- Set a pace. Then have students read the whole words in each task and column.
- Provide repeated practice, building accuracy first, then fluency.

4. Tricky Words

Have students read each row for accuracy, then read the entire grid for fluency.

5. Multisyllabic Words

For each word, have students read each syllable out loud, finger count the syllables, then tell how many syllables are in the word. If needed, use the word in a sentence. Have students read the whole word.

6. Dictation

ate, late, later, plain, rain, train

- Say "ate." Have students say the word. Guide students as they finger count and say the sounds. Have students touch or write the sounds, then read the word. Say something like:

  The first word is ***ate.*** Say the word. (ate)
  Say and count the sounds in ***ate*** with me.

  Hold up one finger for each sound. /āāā/•/t/ How many sounds? (two)

  What's the first sound? (/āāā/) Write /āāā/.
  What's the last sound? (/t/) Touch under /t/.
  Read the word. (ate)
  Yes, the Bossy E at the end makes letter a say its name.

- Repeat with "late" and "later."
- Continue with the rhyming words: plain, rain, train.

EXTRA PRACTICE 3

Unit 8 Decoding Practice

Name ______________________

1. SOUND REVIEW Use selected Sound Cards from Units 1–8.

2. SOUNDING OUT SMOOTHLY Have students say the underlined part, sound out and read each word, then read the row.

wait	poof	house	corn

3. ACCURACY/FLUENCY BUILDING Have students say any underlined part, then read each word. Next, have students read the column.

A1 Mixed Practice	B1 Word Endings	C1 Bossy E	D1 Related Words
know	rub	make	cold
knew	rubbed	share	colder
phone		gave	coldest
Ralph	started		**D2 Compound Words**
threw	decided	rice	something
blue		invite	without
gather	happened	arrive	everyone
dinner	appeared		maybe
rubber	turned	huge	
		stone	
	picked	here	
	walked		

4. TRICKY WORDS Have students read each row for accuracy, then fluency.

A	special	money	only	nothing	pretty	5
B	color	delicious	taught	carry	couldn't	10

5. MULTISYLLABIC WORDS Have students read the word by parts, tell how many syllables are in the word, then read the whole word.

A	hes•i•tate	hesitate	to•geth•er	together
B	im•por•tant	important	sud•den•ly	suddenly
C	um•brel•la	umbrella	E•liz•a•beth	Elizabeth

6. DICTATION Say the word. Have students say the word, then finger count and say the sounds. Have students say each sound as they touch or write it.

A1 Shifty Words	B1 Rhyming Words
a t e	p l a i n
l a t e	r a i n
l a t e r	t r a i n

PROCEDURES

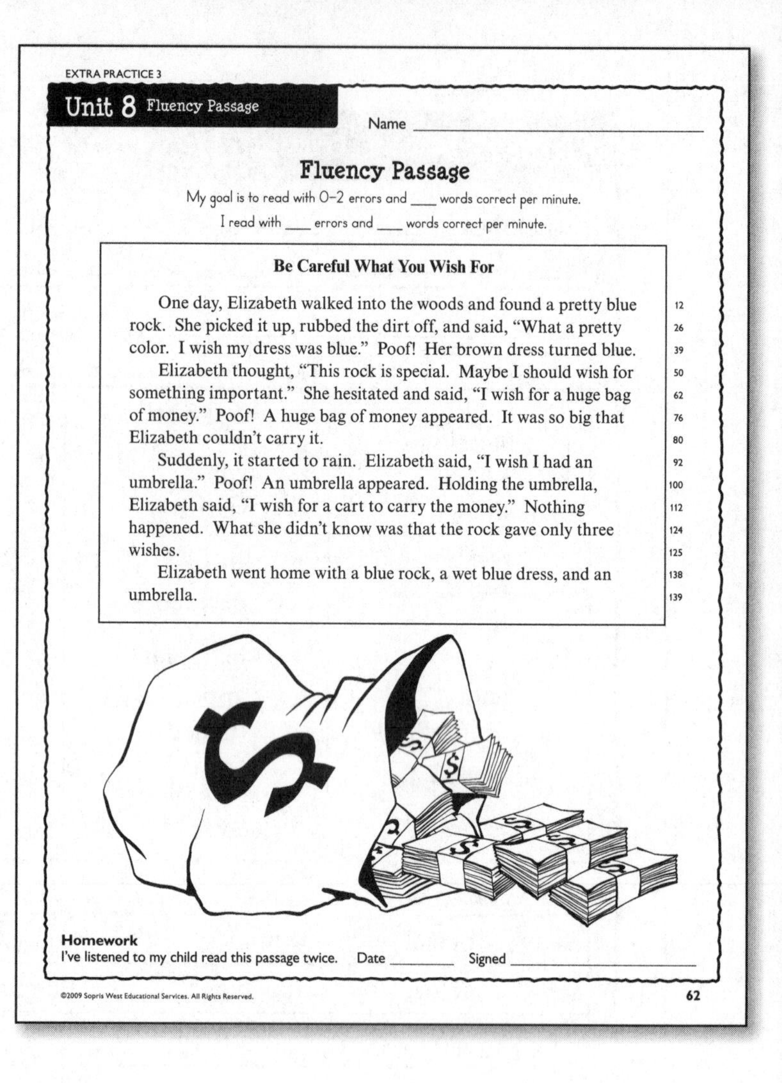

EXTRA PRACTICE 3

Unit 8 Fluency Passage

Name ______

Fluency Passage

My goal is to read with 0–2 errors and ___ words correct per minute.

I read with ___ errors and ___ words correct per minute.

Be Careful What You Wish For

One day, Elizabeth walked into the woods and found a pretty blue rock. She picked it up, rubbed the dirt off, and said, "What a pretty color. I wish my dress was blue." Poof! Her brown dress turned blue. 12 26 39

Elizabeth thought, "This rock is special. Maybe I should wish for something important." She hesitated and said, "I wish for a huge bag of money." Poof! A huge bag of money appeared. It was so big that Elizabeth couldn't carry it. 50 62 76 80

Suddenly, it started to rain. Elizabeth said, "I wish I had an umbrella." Poof! An umbrella appeared. Holding the umbrella, Elizabeth said, "I wish for a cart to carry the money." Nothing happened. What she didn't know was that the rock gave only three wishes. 92 100 112 124 125

Elizabeth went home with a blue rock, a wet blue dress, and an umbrella. 138 139

Homework
I've listened to my child read this passage twice. Date ______ Signed ______

©2009 Sopris West Educational Services. All Rights Reserved. 62

1. **First Reading**
   Mix group and individual turns, independent of your voice. Have students work toward an accuracy goal of 0–2 errors and practice any difficult words.

2. **Second Reading, Short Passage Practice: Developing Prosody**
   - Demonstrate how to read a line or two with expression. Read at a rate slightly faster than the students' rate. Say something like:
     Listen as I read the first two sentences with expression and phrasing. I'm going to emphasize certain words and pause between sentences.
     "One day, Elizabeth walked into the woods and found a pretty blue rock. She picked it up, rubbed the dirt off, and said, 'What a pretty color.'"
   - Guide practice with your voice.
     Now read the paragraph with me.
   - Provide individual turns while others track with their fingers and whisper read. Provide descriptive and positive feedback.
     [Anand], you read with wonderful expression!

3. **Partner Reading: Repeated Reading (Checkout Opportunity)**

While students do Partner Reading, listen to individuals read the passage. Work on accuracy and fluency, as needed.

4. **Homework: Repeated Reading**

Have students read the story at home.

PROCEDURES

For each step, demonstrate and guide practice, as needed. Then have students complete the page independently.

1. Activity

Passage Comprehension

- Have students read each sentence or question, then fill in the bubble with the correct answer.
- Think aloud with students and discuss the multiple-choice options, as needed.

Paragraph Comprehension

- Have students read the paragraph.
- Have students read each numbered sentence or question, then fill in the bubble and/or blank, or check the correct answer.
- Have students read the completed sentence.

Self-monitoring

Have students read and check their work, then draw a happy face in the Check and Correct circle.

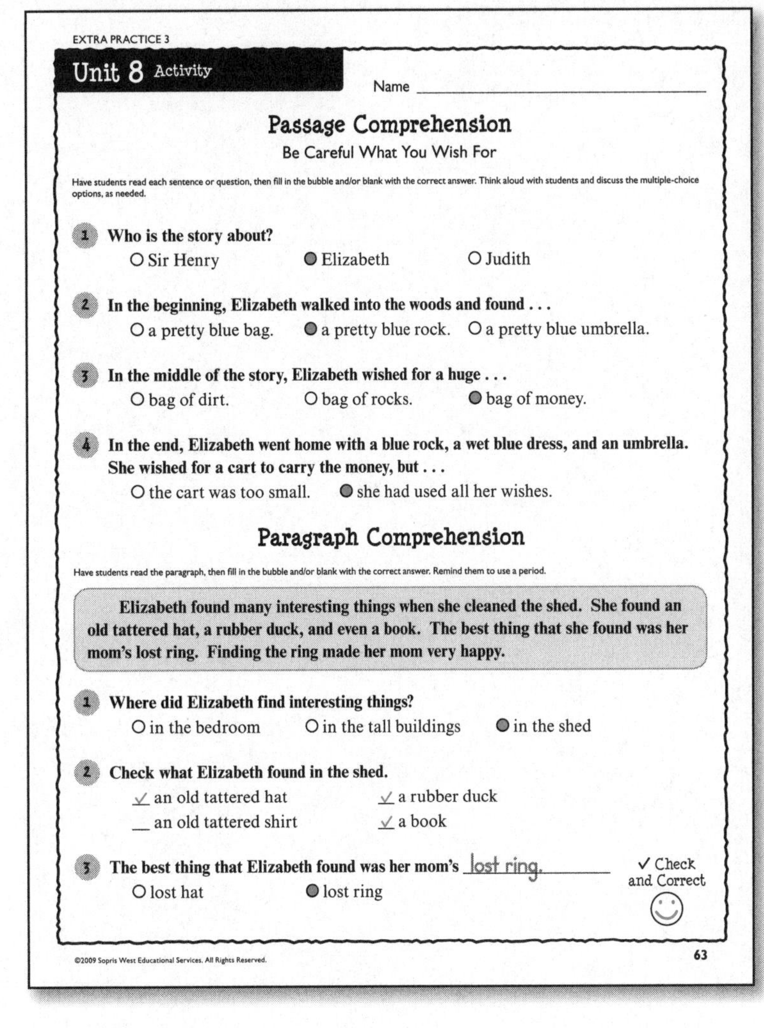

EXTRA PRACTICE 3

Unit 8 Activity

Name ______________

Passage Comprehension

Be Careful What You Wish For

Have students read each sentence or question, then fill in the bubble and/or blank with the correct answer. Think aloud with students and discuss the multiple-choice options, as needed.

1. **Who is the story about?**
   ○ Sir Henry ● Elizabeth ○ Judith

2. **In the beginning, Elizabeth walked into the woods and found . . .**
   ○ a pretty blue bag. ● a pretty blue rock. ○ a pretty blue umbrella.

3. **In the middle of the story, Elizabeth wished for a huge . . .**
   ○ bag of dirt. ○ bag of rocks. ● bag of money.

4. **In the end, Elizabeth went home with a blue rock, a wet blue dress, and an umbrella. She wished for a cart to carry the money, but . . .**
   ○ the cart was too small. ● she had used all her wishes.

Paragraph Comprehension

Have students read the paragraph, then fill in the bubble and/or blank with the correct answer. Remind them to use a period.

Elizabeth found many interesting things when she cleaned the shed. She found an old tattered hat, a rubber duck, and even a book. The best thing that she found was her mom's lost ring. Finding the ring made her mom very happy.

1. **Where did Elizabeth find interesting things?**
   ○ in the bedroom ○ in the tall buildings ● in the shed

2. **Check what Elizabeth found in the shed.**
   ✓ an old tattered hat ✓ a rubber duck
   __ an old tattered shirt ✓ a book

3. **The best thing that Elizabeth found was her mom's** lost ring.
   ○ lost hat ● lost ring

✓ Check and Correct ☺

63

2. Word Fluency (BLMs are located on the CD.)

You may wish to have students repeat practice with Extra Practice, Word Fluency A or B.

Teacher's Guide

UNIT 8

Level 2
166916
ISBN-13: 978-1-60218-531-9
ISBN-10: 1-60218-531-X
9 781602 185319

Sopris West®
EDUCATIONAL SERVICES
A Cambium Learning® Company